The Complete Photo Guide to

CARDMAKING

Quarto is the authority on a wide range of topics.

Quarto educates, entertains and enriches the lives of our readers—enthusiasts and lovers of hands-on living.

www.QuartoKnows.com

First published in the United States of America by
Creative Publishing international, an imprint of
Quarto Publishing Group USA Inc.
400 First Avenue North
Suite 400
Minneapolis, MN 55401
1-800-328-3895
QuartoKnows.com
Visit our blogs at QuartoKnows.com.

ISBN: 978-1-58923-882-4

Digital edition published in 2015
eISBN: 978-1-6278-825-7

10 9 8 7 6 5 4 3 2

Library of Congress Cataloging-in-Publication Data available

Copy Editor: Karen Levy
Proofreader: Ron Hampton
Page Layout: Laurie L. Young
Photographs: Rob Bostick and Judi Watanabe

Printed in China

The Complete Photo Guide to
CARDMAKING

Creative Publishing
international

CONTENTS

Introduction

I'm not sure when I fell in love with making cards, but I suspect it had something to do with all the cards given to me as a child. The first I can remember is when I had my tonsils removed and I had to spend the night in the hospital. Mrs. Holmquist brought a basket of hand-drawn "get well wishes" from my classmates. I especially loved the pink crepe-paper carnation glued to the purple construction paper. Those brightly colored, funnily illustrated, wonderful heartfelt messages brightened my day, and I still smile when I think about them.

Maybe I liked receiving these cards because of the mailman who delivered them to me. He knew my sisters and me by name and he would say, "Judi, I think there's a card in here for you." Maybe I fell in love with cards because I associated them with the people and events that make me feel warm, happy, and sometimes fuzzy ("With Love and Warm Fuzzies" was the greeting on one of the cards I happily remember).

At some point, I started making the cards I was giving away. Probably because Mom thought the volume of cards and letters I was purchasing and sending was becoming extreme. So a budget cut was in order, and she encouraged me to "make it myself." That became a new adventure—how to make my own cards with what I could find around the house. Card stock came from the stiff sheets of paper used in the packaging from my sisters' tights. Scissors were the kiddie style, with the rounded tip that cut only 2 inches (5 cm) at a time. This was a little disappointing because they left my paper with jagged and sometimes torn edges. One day, I discovered my mom's dressmaking shears. I cut a stack of paper and was pleased with my work. My mom was not as pleased. Apparently, cutting paper with scissors intended for fabric dulls the blades. Later, she bought me a special pair of paper-cutting scissors. I still use these today. I found that having the right tool for the job helped me make cards that looked professional, but they also made my cards easy to make. My efforts were always rewarded. I continue to be encouraged by the compliments returned when my cards are received. To make sure my recipients know that the cards are hand crafted, I mark my cards with my personalized signature. After all, a handmade card is truly a message from your heart.

A BRIEF HISTORY

While gathering ideas for different cardmaking styles and techniques, I wondered who started making and giving cards? The ancient Chinese are credited for this custom. They started exchanging cards decorated with well-wishing messages when celebrating the New Year. Other cultures adopted this tradition, but giving handmade cards was considered a luxury. When mechanized printing became the standard (1850s), greeting cards were produced mechanically in volume. About the same time, the postage stamp was introduced, and the inexpensive method of postal delivery made card giving more affordable and popular.

Today, cardmaking continues to be popular, and the giving of handmade cards makes this tradition special. Materials to make cards are plentiful, and finding beautiful and unusual papers along with the right tools adds to the enthusiasm for this hobby. Receiving a beautifully handmade greeting card will always present the most sincere sentiment. (Sources: The Greeting Card Association, *Paper Crafts* magazine, the Craft & Hobby Association.)

CARDMAKING BASICS

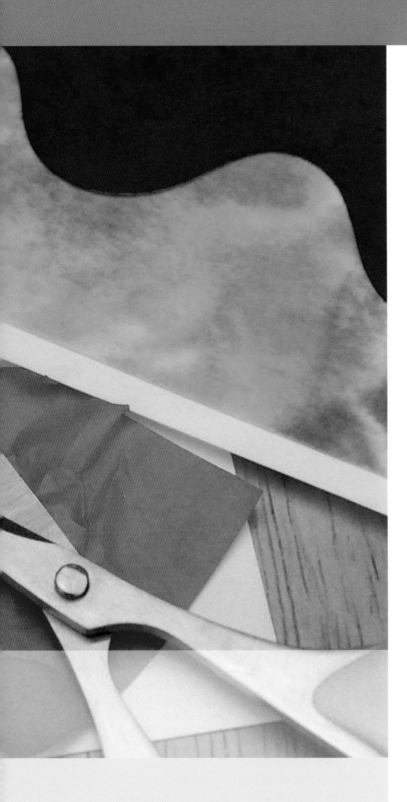

Making cards can be as easy or as complicated as you wish. You need only a few tools that can be easily made or purchased. These few demonstration photos and simple instructions will show you clearly how to use these tools.

But before doing anything, the most important piece of information you need is how will your card be delivered? Will you deliver it yourself, or will you send it in the mail? Once you determine this, then you can decide what size to make your cards. If you wish to hand deliver your card, then any size is possible. However, if your cards are to be delivered by the U.S. Postal Service, then it is easiest and most cost effective to make cards that fit standard-size envelopes. Once you determine the size of card you wish to make, the fun starts.

Tools

There are a few tools that make cardmaking a snap. They range from the inexpensive to the finest crafted quality tools. Remember, these tools only make the process of making cards by hand easier; they do not change the message that a handmade card delivers. Anything you make will always send a sincere message.

BASIC TOOLS

Cardmaking tools are plentiful and can range from things you find in your household toolbox to items you purchase at your local craft supply store. A shop specializing in scrapbooking or paper arts will have most everything you need without having to search the racks.

Scissors

Straight-Edged Scissors

Using a nice quality pair of scissors assures a clean, crisp cut. It is best to have separate shears or scissors for paper and fabric. I like keeping two pairs of scissors close at hand. One is a 6-inch (15 cm) blade. This allows me to cut longer lengths easily. The second pair is a smaller 2-inch (5 cm) blade that cuts finer detail with precision and ease.

Decorative Scissors

A wide variety of decorative cutting edges are available to enhance cards. These scissors will generally cut through all papers, although thicker papers may be beyond the limitation of these decorative edges.

Rulers

Straight edges can be made from anything sturdy and straight—wood, scraps of mat board, the edge of a cereal box all make straight edges. Rulers are helpful when drawing guidelines for card layouts and helping to write your message on a straight line. For those that prefer cards with a more organic look, a ruler can be used to tear the edge of the paper, creating a faux deckle, or decorative, edge. Rulers are available with imperial (inches) or metric (centimeters) measurements.

Steel-Edged Rulers

Made from wood or plastic and steel, these rulers have a piece of metal (steel) embedded in one side of the ruler that makes a precise, durable edge. Gouging or cutting into the plastic or wood is extremely difficult when using the steel side of the ruler, thus preventing accidental nicks or indentations that cause the ruler to be unusable.

Clear Rulers

These rulers made from plastic or acrylic are nice because they generally have a printed grid or guidelines. Perpendicular cuts can be made using the vertical lines on the ruler. Often these grid-marked rulers also have a "zero find," which is a nice tool for finding the center of a card.

Craft or Hobby Knife

There are many different cutting tools for cardmaking, and the type of cutting knife for your cards depends on the detail of the cutouts you plan to make as well as the thickness of the paper you are cutting. A thick paper cuts nicely with a sturdier blade, while thinner papers need only a sharp but precise blade.

Some of the most popular craft knives use a disposable blade that can be removed by loosening the blade holder. A sharp craft blade is the key to a smooth cut line. Plus, you are less likely to cut yourself if your blade cuts through the paper easily. If you have to add extra pressure to cut the paper, there is a chance you can slip. So use caution.

Precision Craft Knife

Generally, this style of knife is made from an aluminum handle with a collet (a holding device or chuck) that tightens to securely hold the knife blade. Often the handles are covered with a rubberized grip that helps when using for long periods of time.

Penknife

This craft knife looks like a pen and the blade retracts like the point of a ballpoint pen. It makes cutting curved lines relatively easy because you draw the blade along a line as if you were tracing the line with a pen. It is especially easy to cut straight lines when used with a steel-edged ruler. Be careful to use an even amount of pressure while cutting. With too much pressure you could cut through everything, including your work surface or table. Generally, the best amount of pressure is approximately the amount of pressure used when squishing a gummy candy.

Cutting Mat

It is wise to use a cutting mat to protect your work area. A self-healing cutting mat is made from a high-density vinyl that is hard yet has a little flex. When you cut into the mat, the cuts appear to heal and you do not see the cut lines left in the mat. Cutting mats often have printed guidelines that help for layout and measuring. They also cushion the surface when applying eyelet embellishments.

Bone Folder

After taking a class in bookbinding, I learned the value of a bone folder and how useful it is for cardmaking. By scoring the paper *before* folding it, you create a line where the paper will easily fold. It is quite magical because you can also draw a curved line with the pointed side of the bone folder and the paper will fold along the curved line. This is how dimensional paper petals for flowers are created.

The most popular folding tools are made from bone, although there are folders also made from plastic. The bone is hard enough to dent the paper, creating the scored lines. The pointed end should be pointy but not sharp or it can tear or pierce the paper while scoring. The rounded lengthwise sides have a smooth curve, so applying pressure to the scored fold makes a crisp fold. These rounded edges also slide easily along scored lines, eliminating drag when scoring stacks of paper.

OTHER FUN AND HELPFUL TOOLS

You may find after making a variety of cards that your tastes, creativity, and skills open the door for other tools. If you are making large multiples of cards, these tools can be incredibly helpful.

Cutters or Trimmers

Mechanical cutting tools like paper cutters or trimmers are very handy. A simple alignment with the tool's built-in ruler creates a nicely cut card. All cutter styles have their positive and negative features, but they all cut precisely if used properly.

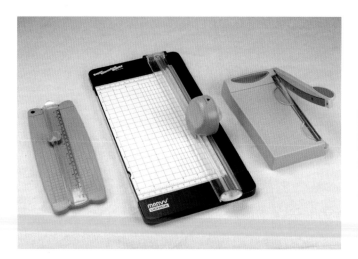

Guillotine Cutter

These cutters have a blade mounted on an arm (knife) and a stationary blade attached to the base of the cutting table edge. The knife is drawn along the edge of the cutting surface in a scissorlike motion. For accuracy, it is important to securely hold the paper with the attached safety guard while cutting. Generally, there is no need to replace the blade; however, heavier duty cutters have blades that can be sharpened. Large guillotine cutters are made from wood or metal and they can cut through thick sheets of paper or multiple sheets at one time. However, they are heavy, expensive, and take up space. Smaller, more economical guillotine cutters that are made from plastic with thinner steel blades sit conveniently on your desk or fit neatly in a drawer.

Rotary Cutters

This tool has a blade attached to a shuttle that glides along a rail. Though lightweight and compact, it and can cut up to 100 lb. card stock with ease. Rotary cutters are easy to use and, on some models, you have the option to switch to shaped blades. Often cuts are accurate without holding the paper securely in place because the cutting blade slides along the guide bar. The actual amount of friction on the paper is minor, so there is not as much pull. The blades and the plastic cutting bars are replaceable.

Scoring Boards

These tools help to precisely score papers for a crisp, clean fold. There are several different styles and all are helpful when making scored lines. Specially designed boards have either molded guidelines and grids or a raised metal bar with a special scoring tool. Both have a lip or stop to help align the paper for precise scored lines.

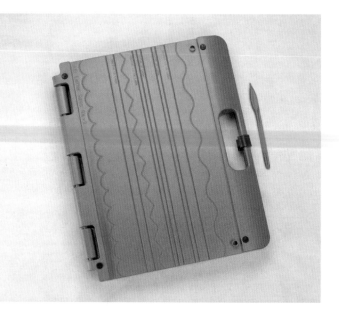

Punches

Punched holes or cutouts in your cards create a nice detail or addition to the composition of your work. The most popular punch is a circle or hole punch, but there are many different shapes, sizes, and styles of punches available. These punches or shaped cutouts can be used to make little windows, appliqué shapes, and even confetti.

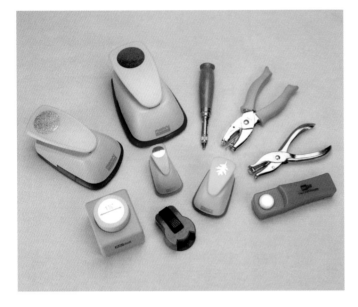

Hole Punch

These handheld punches are available in a wide range of diameters as well as strength (how strong it's made). Some punches will create holes in paper as thick as 2 mm; however, the most common punches work nicely with normal cardstock-weight papers.

Standard Office Supply Punch This is the perfect size to make a ¼-inch (6 mm) hole in your card stock or paper. Holes are punched within a 1-inch (2.5 cm) margin from the edge of the paper.

Long-Reach Hole Punch Some punches are called "long reach." These punches are designed so a hole can be punched 3 or 4 inches (7.5 or 10 cm) from the edge, making it possible to make a hole in the middle of a postcard-size piece of paper.

Screw Punch These punches, also called Japanese screw punches, are on the must-have tool list for bookbinders. It's a little overkill for cardmakers, but this is a tool that I find useful when the long-reach hole punch will not create a hole where I want one. These tools can punch through card stock, fabric, vellum, leather, and even softer plastics. It makes a nice hole through thicknesses up to several millimeters deep, which is great when you want to punch through several sheets of paper at once.

Shapes and Border Punches

Available from several manufacturers, shaped punches add a fun dimension to your cardmaking by creating shaped cutouts or windows with speed and ease. There are many different shapes in a wide variety of sizes. Some of these shaped punches are extremely detailed and make your handmade cards look like they were made by someone who has an incredible talent with scissors. While most of these shaped cutouts can be achieved using a pair of scissors or a penknife, punches are perfect when you want to duplicate the shape or pattern multiple times.

Cutting Machines

Often punching paper can tire your hands, especially when the number of punched images becomes excessive. This is where cutting machines are helpful. There are two basic styles: roller and computerized.

Personal Roller Cutters

Card stock or paper is sandwiched between layers of plastic shims, along with a shaped die or cutter. The die has a sharp edge, which cuts through the paper. A handle is used to crank the paper through the machine. Pressure is applied and the shape is cut. Each manufacturer has a unique formula for layering their shims and dies. These all vary and depend on the thickness of the paper or material being cut. Some manufacturers have added a motor to automatically crank the paper, giving your arm a rest.

Computerized Plotter Cutting Machines

For those who feel comfortable using a computer, electronic cutting machines are available. Just like printing a document from your desktop computer, these machines allow you to use both predesigned templates or your own design to create cutout shapes.

Materials

Materials for making cards are plentiful and can be found everywhere: your desk, the recycle bin, even the medicine cabinet. Fortunately, you can also purchase materials almost everywhere: at the grocery, office-supply, and even department stores. The bonanza of cardmaking materials, however, can be found in craft stores, especially those that specialize in paper crafts.

PAPER

While it is possible to make cards with all types of materials, the most popular and probably easiest material to use is paper. It is ubiquitous and ranges from sheets that are relatively inexpensive to those that rival the best-quality fabrics. There are many different types of paper, but generally paper can be divided into a few categories. Knowing the type of paper will help when choosing different adhesives, coloring media, and types of cutting tools. You can even use paper to convey the mood of your message. For example, a brightly colored smooth paper may say "Let's celebrate," and a natural handmade paper may say "Relax, be peaceful."

Weight and Thickness

Paper is available in a range of weights or thickness. Commercially produced papers follow a standard—one for the United States and another (international) for everyone else. Sometimes, Japanese paper companies use a standard that is a slight variation from the international standard. Thickness is measured by caliper and is usually presented in thousandths of an inch (U.S.) or millimeters (international). However, the more predominant identification for paper thickness is the weight of the paper. A popular weight for card stock is 80 pounds (lb) or 160 grams (g). Text-weight paper is lighter and used for books and stationery. You can find this labeled as 20 to 24 lb or 60 to 120 g.

Commercially handmade papers are made from a wide variety of natural fibers from many different countries. Their weights or thicknesses vary, due to their handmade quality, but they are made within a range from thicker papers to featherweight papers like tissue paper. Thicker paper is normally used for the base of a card, and thinner paper is used for layers or appliqué. These papers also have various textures that can enhance the beauty of your cards.

An offshoot of making cards by hand is making the paper for your cards as well. It is a relatively simple process, but some equipment is needed. Also, there are papermaking kits available. Because papermaking involves water, it is a fun project to do outside in the summer.

Paper Surfaces

Paper is available with a wide range of surfaces, from smooth to textured. For most of the cards created for this book, papers can be used "as is." But if you wish to paint, rubber stamp, or color the paper as part of your handmade card, a little knowledge about the surface of the paper will help ensure you achieve the best results. The paper's surface also helps you make decisions about the types of adhesive to use when assembling your cards. Smoother paper works great with any form of adhesive. It also provides an even surface for writing with pens that use fluid inks—dip pens, fountain and technical pens, and marking pens.

Coated Paper

Generally speaking, coated papers are those that have a layer or coating and fall into the category of smoother papers. Sometimes, these layers are made from nonporous products like laminated plastics. The laminate provides a barrier to liquids that helps protect the paper from spills. However, these surfaces will also repel ink, should you wish to paint or write on the card, although permanent or alcohol-based inks will work. Other coatings include smooth applications of materials like clay. This creates a nice surface that is slightly absorbent, which allows inks to dry without bleeding or feathering, creating a crisp image.

Uncoated Paper

Papers without a coating are nice to use because they look and feel organic and natural. Most of these papers have relatively smooth finishes and sometimes have a slight texture. These textured papers are created when a screen or sieve is used in the production process. The paper takes on the texture of the screen. Originally, this surface was called a "laid" surface and had very fine horizontal lines. At some point, a more symmetrical screen was used, giving these papers the appearance of a woven or linen texture and it became known as a "linen" surface. Textured surfaces work well for cardmaking and bring a nice element without any extra effort.

Handmade Paper

Handmade papers are part of the uncoated paper category but with a more textured surface. These papers can have rough textures, resembling objects from the bark of a tree to smoother surfaces that almost look like lace. These papers add depth and dimension to your work and can be used alone without added decoration. However, as the texture becomes more dimensional, it is important to use adhesives that are really sticky. Because handmade papers are generally more absorbent, paste and liquid adhesives can soak into the paper, which is only a problem if it changes the appearance of the paper.

Paper Grain

Paper has a grain. This is the alignment of the fibers that make up the paper. Knowing the grain direction is important because paper will crack if folded across the grain. Papers can curl if wet adhesives or paints are applied. Ironing the paper after the paint has dried helps flatten the curl. Also, layering different pieces and applying them perpendicularly helps to naturally flatten your work.

Paper fed into a machine will bend around rollers. It is important to know the direction of the grain so the paper can be properly inserted into machines such as a printing press, photocopier, or typewriter. Paper should be fed grain side first so that the axis of the rollers is along the grain.

How to Identify the Grain Direction

Loosely hold a sheet of card stock with both hands. Slightly bend the paper. Turn it 90 degrees and slightly bend it again. The grain runs parallel to the bend with least resistance.

Paper Sizes

Machine-made papers come in standard sizes. This is so sheets of paper are uniform and will work with both desktop and large professional printing presses with few mechanical malfunctions or paper jams. Generally, paper sizes are divided by regions—the United States and international (with several countries having slight variations on the international standard). The traditional North American inch-based sizes are "letter," "legal," "ledger," and "tabloid," are these are measured in inches. Letter-size paper is the most commonly used size. The origins of the exact dimensions of "letter" size paper (8½ x 11 inches, or 21.6 x 28 cm) are lost in tradition and not well documented.

This standard has been set so commercial printers can use machinery that is basically the same, allowing for efficiency in the printing process. These sizes have been worked into the personal printers you use at home. This size of paper (USA letter or international A4) is often the base for handmade cards because it is the most common cut of paper available to consumers.

International paper sizes are based on metric measurements. The A series is the most popular paper standard (with measurements based on a formula that involves algebra). For a cardmaker's purpose, I use the more practical information, knowing that everything is based on folding the paper in half. This makes it easy to design cards. The most popular size is A4, which is used widely in the same way that the letter size is very common in the U.S.

The only reason why paper size is important to a cardmaker is because paper sizes are used to determine envelope sizes. Envelopes are important because postage services have set guidelines for postage rates based on preestablished envelope sizes. Although you can mail any size envelope, the best price postage is for standard-size envelopes.

ENVELOPES

The simplest way to package or protect a greeting card is with an envelope. They are made from all types of paper and plastics and can be found in a variety of sizes. It is best to use standard-size envelopes because additional postage is required for odd-sized or -shaped envelopes. Thicker or bulkier envelopes might be classified as packages but will be safely delivered with the proper postage. The U.S. Postal Service is incredible because they will deliver any item as long as it has proper postage and annotations. However, they prefer standard sizes because these are processed efficiently within their machinery, making the system run smoothly.

As a new cardmaker, I made cards based on the paper I had. Sometimes, the paper was a scrap from a larger piece, but generally this was not a standard size. I quickly discovered there might not be a standard envelope that fit my card. So I made my own. Luckily, most of my homemade envelopes fit within the postal service guidelines for normal postage and most were delivered without mishap. However, after a catastrophic delivery —my handmade card and envelope sent to a friend in Germany arrived as several torn pieces in a plastic bag—I now understand that sturdy paper and a good strong adhesive helps ensure the safe delivery of my little works of art.

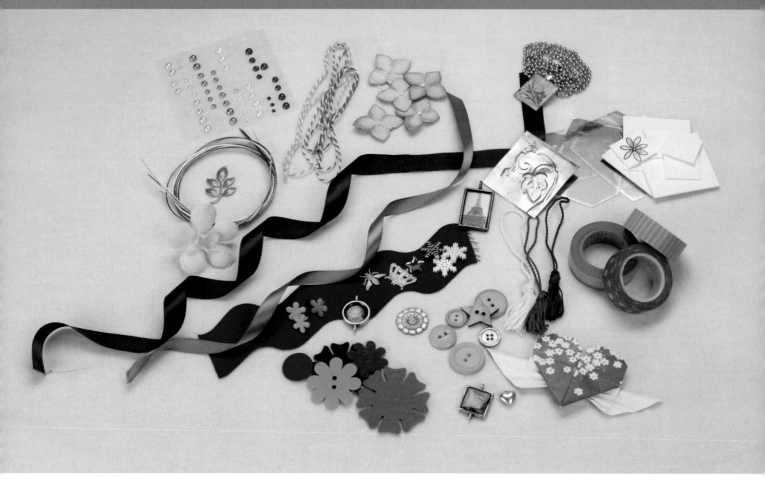

EMBELLISHMENTS

These little added elements bring dimension, color, elegance, and even whimsy. Embellishments vary from sophisticated to quirky and can be both memorable and treasured. It can be part of your message or just something bright and shiny that makes you feel good.

ADHESIVES

This is the "glue that holds everything together." There are many different ways to adhere the parts of your cards and little works of art. The type of adhesive used depends on the materials you are using.

Wet or Paste Adhesives

Wet glues are nice for securing layers on your cards as well as applying embellishments. A popular adhesive is polyvinyl acetate (PVA). It is water based, easy to use, and easy to clean up. There are other solvent-based

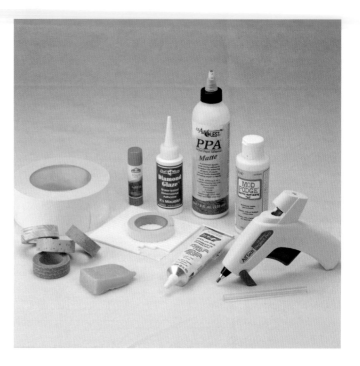

adhesives that work on paper, but be sure to test, as some of the liquid soaks into and discolors the paper or items you're adhering. Paste is a thicker wet adhesive. Historically speaking, many of these pastes were made with household items like rice or wheat flour mixed with water. Although they are easy to use, they could be detrimental to the longevity of your work. Often, little bugs eat this paste and then sometimes eat your work as well.

Dry Adhesives

Professionals generally prefer these methods of adhering materials because they are often cleaner to use. They are available in a few categories, and some require extra tools; however, most can be used by anyone.

Heat-Activated Dry Adhesives

These need an iron or some kind of heat activation. Photographers use dry mount boards that are coated with a glue that was dried in manufacturing. To adhere the photograph to a mat board for framing, photographers secure the photo to the board using a gigantic heat press.

Beeswax

Beeswax was used centuries ago to secure embellishments to decorations on furniture and walls. While beeswax alone will glue objects together, a combination of beeswax and resin makes a more durable adhesive. Often used to seal documents, a dollop of beeswax impressed with a stamp was how senders and receivers were assured their correspondence was secure. If the seal was broken, then the recipient knew the document had been opened.

Double-Sided Tape

There are many different types of tape. For cardmaking purposes, double-sided pressure-sensitive tapes are great because the tape is hidden behind the layer you are securing. I like using tape that is sticky but still allows repositioning if lightly placed on my cards, yet is secure once pressed into position.

Decorative Tape

I can't leave out colored and printed tapes. Most commonly known as masking tape and, today, washi tape, these tapes were originally colored to help categorize the

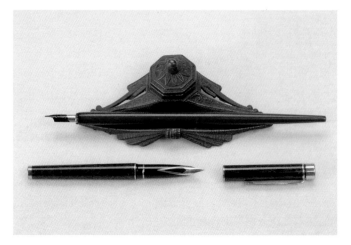

level of stickiness of the adhesive. Today, tape manufacturers make hundreds of printed and colored decorative tapes in several widths. Decorative tape may be considered an embellishment as well as an adhesive, making it doubly useful.

WRITING TOOLS

Every card needs a message, and the most personal messages (I believe) are handwritten. The writing instrument used is a personal preference, but somehow using a nice "feel good" pen or pencil seems to make you, well, feel good.

Pencils

Temporary marks made with a pencil are nice because you can erase them if you make a mistake. Both graphite and colored pencils are nice for children, especially when little mistakes should be corrected. Sometimes, a colored pencil gives you a nice subtle blending that yields a quiet, calm feeling to your message.

Pens

Pens are the most common tool used to handwrite a message in a greeting card because they are permanent. You wouldn't want the recipient to think that you might change your mind about the message. A handwritten note is very special. Don't worry if your penmanship is illegible, your handwritten message is one from your heart. However, if you truly need a cryptologist to read your writing, then a typed message is better than no message.

COLORING TOOLS

Most greeting cards are colorful. Color adds meaning to your message. While colored paper is part of the card, coloring tools are also important. There are many ways to add color to your work, and often you can mix and match to create just the effect you want.

Markers

Markers have broad tips that quickly and neatly apply ink. It is similar to a paintbrush with paint, yet very different because the ink is stored in the barrel of the pen, making it convenient and clean.

Water-Based Markers

These markers use a dye-based ink, which cleans off fingers with soap and water. It is perfect for children and adults who love bright, vibrant colors.

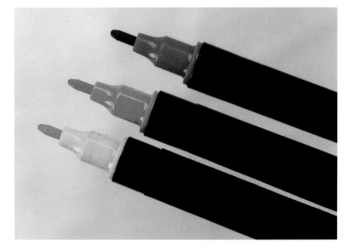

Permanent Ink Markers

These use solvent-based inks, which are waterproof and mostly permanent on your paper. Just know that when using these markers, this type of ink can be tricky to remove from tabletops, walls, and pretty little dresses.

Always Have the Right Color

Sometimes, I find I need a particular color of a material or an object (such as a brad or flower). With a broad collection of permanent ink marker colors, you can change the wrong-colored object to the right one.

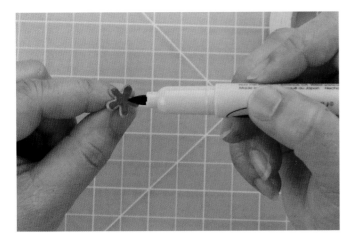

Metallic Markers

Available in both water-based and permanent, these bright and shiny markers finish the card nicely if you need a little "pop."

White Pens and Markers

These pens are nice when you are working on dark paper. You can also add a highlight to a dark object to give it a little more dimension, and in some cases, cover up a very small boo boo.

Paint

Generally, paint is made from pigments held together with different liquids: water, oil, or acrylic. The higher grades of paint are often classified as archival because the pigments are truly found in nature and change very little with age or environment. Synthetic pigments are more economical and may change with time. However, even inexpensive paints will often hold their color, especially when the card is stored away from UV light. Paint can be a big category, but for cardmaking, water-based paints are the most convenient and easy to use.

Watercolor

Watercolor paint is readily available and easy to use for all ages. You need only a little water and a piece of paper to get started. Artist-quality watercolors are generally more expensive because they are made mostly from pigment, giving intense and brightly colored results. For greeting cards, a little goes a long way.

Acrylic Paint

Acrylics are also water based, and for cardmaking they are easy to use and clean up. Unlike watercolor, acrylic paints are more permanent after they dry. That is, you can re-wet watercolors and some of the paint will lift off. If you re-wet acrylic paint, the paint remains.

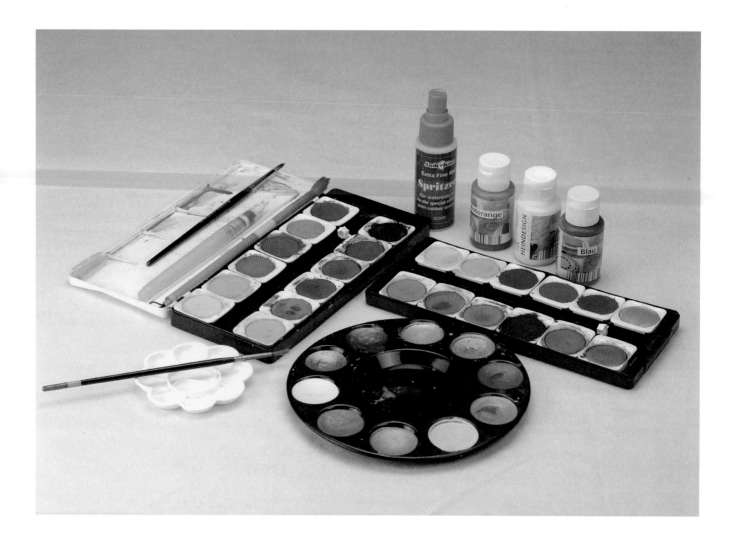

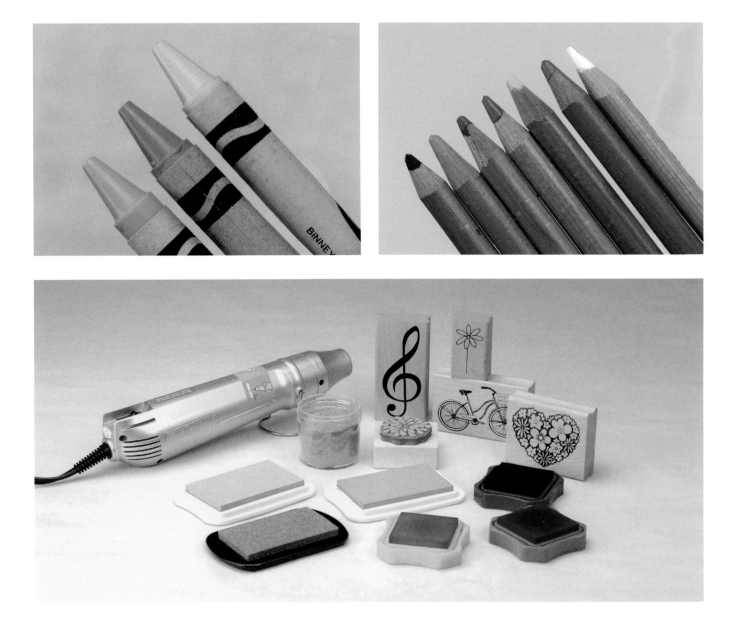

Crayons

These are great to use for a quick addition of color and are especially fun for children. No mess, no fuss.

Colored Pencils

Available in all levels of quality and variety of colors, colored pencils are easy to use. Like crayons, there is no need for water or inks, and they can be used on most paper surfaces. Uncoated card stock works best.

Ink Pads

With a wide selection of colors and types of inks, ink pads let you create almost any color of paper needed for your cards. Use them directly on the paper itself or more conveniently use with a rubber stamp. There are so many possibilities for this great "eye candy."

Skills

There are a few skills that will help make your cards little works of art. For example, knowing how best to hold a pair of scissors will make cutting out pieces easy and enjoyable. Understanding the markings on a ruler will ensure the focus of your card will be in the center, and these marks can help you make your cards look more professional. Overall, the skills for cardmaking are easy to master, allowing you to explore your creative side.

MEASURING

Counting fractions and using a ruler can seem like math. For some people, this is not fun. There are many references to fractions in this book, and though it may seem intimidating, it is not. If you know just a couple of tricks, this type of math is fun. Of all the things you need to measure, calculating the center of the card is important. Once you understand this, the rest is easy.

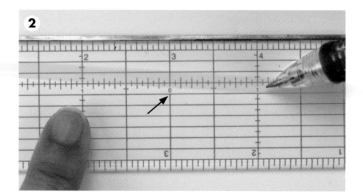

How to Find the Center of the Paper

1 Look for the zero marked in the center of the ruler.

2 Notice the measurements to the right and left of the zero. These are indicated by units that are marked as 1, 2, and 3 and fractions of these measurements.

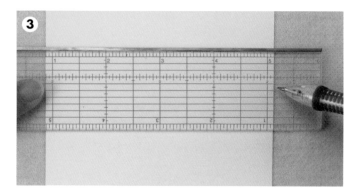

3 Place the ruler approximately in the center of the page and align the right and left sides, matching the numbers to the left and right of the ruler. For example, if the paper is 6 inches (15 cm) wide, you will align the number "3" on the left and right edges.

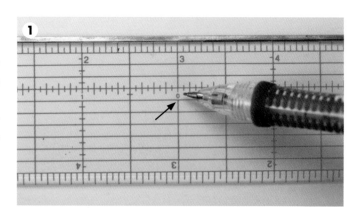

4 The zero point is in the center of the page.

5 To draw a guideline for the center of the card, mark two separate points at the zero mark. Turn the ruler 90 degrees and connect the dots.

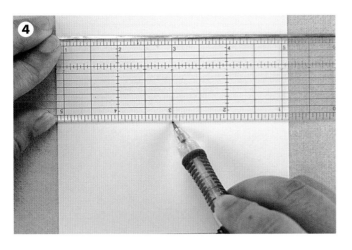

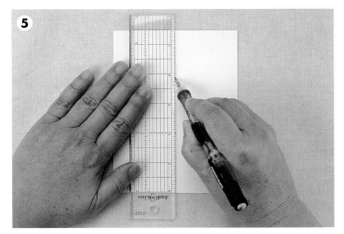

Using the grid guidelines on clear or transparent ruler saves the step of drawing guidelines on the paper.

CUTTING

I'm not sure which comes first: cutting or folding. It's the chicken-and-egg dilemma of cardmaking. In order to have a neat, accurate fold, you need to have a precisely cut piece of paper. But you can create an accurately cut piece of paper if you have one clean fold. Because we need to start somewhere, let's start with cutting.

The easiest way to trim a card is with a pair of scissors. However, trimming a square edge can be difficult even when following a ruled guideline. Using a ruler and craft knife takes a little skill but yields good results. Alternatively, using a compact paper trimmer (either guillotine or rotary) works great if you have one available.

Cutting with a Ruler and Scissors

1 Line up the edge of the ruler and mark where you wish to cut. Repeat so you now have two marks that should be equidistant from the edge.

2 Connect the marks by drawing a line using the ruler.

3 Using a long-bladed pair of scissors, use even pressure and cut along this line.

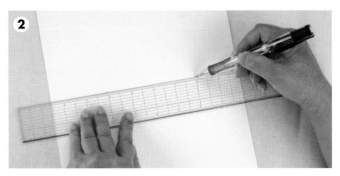

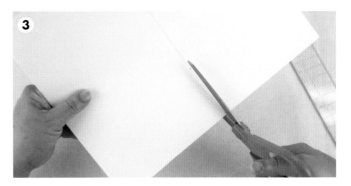

Cutting with a Ruler and Craft Knife

There are many different styles of rulers. The best for cutting directly with a craft knife are rulers that have steel edges.

1 Set your paper on top of a self-healing cutting mat or a cutting board or other surface.

2 Align the ruler at the point on the paper where you wish to cut. Set the tip of the craft knife along the edge of the ruler and, with even pressure, draw the blade toward you.

Cutting with a Guillotine Style of Paper Trimmer

1 Insert the paper into the paper trimmer underneath the finger guard. If the finger guard is flat, hold the guard down to prevent the paper from moving. Note: When this guard is not holding the paper firmly in place, the paper can slip and will cut unevenly.

2 Using constant, even pressure, press the blade closed.

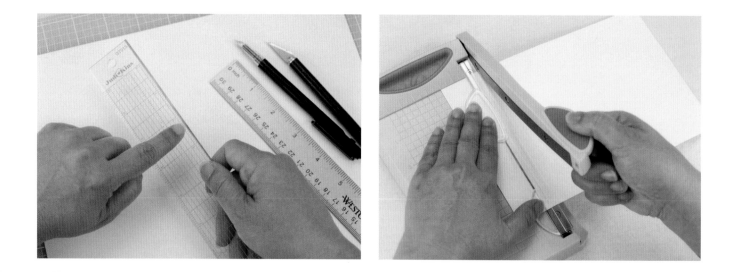

Cutting with a Rotary Style Cutter

1 Insert the paper into the paper trimmer underneath the guide holding the cutting blade.

2 Close the guide and press down while sliding the cutting blade down the length of the paper.

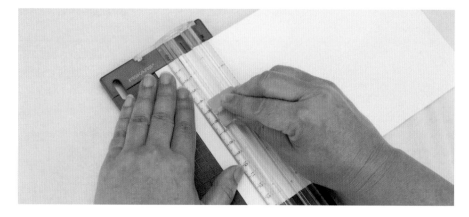

Practice First

It is best to use a thinner sheet of paper to practice, moving to a thicker sheet of card stock once you feel comfortable.

Squaring Up the Card

If you have an asymmetrical piece of paper and its shape is unruly, you can square it up and have the perfect card.

1 Slide the paper into the paper trimmer and cut one side.

2 Turn the cut side and align it with the paper stop (top of the cutter).

3 Continue rotating the paper, aligning each side as you cut. The final card will have nicely squared corners.

Square Up the Card Using the Fold

If you use the fold made by the scoring tool as a guide, you can crop the outside edges of the card and make them square.

1 Align the folded edge along the paper trimmer stop and cut the edges square.

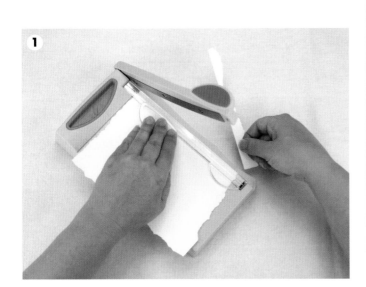

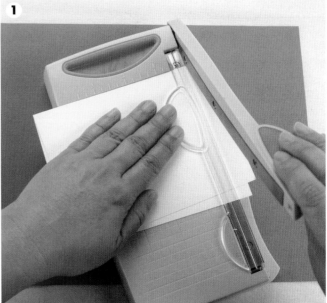

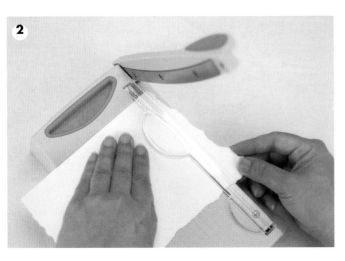

FOLDING

Although it seems that folding a card is simple enough, there are a few subtle details that will take a handmade card from amateur to professional. Tools as simple as a bone folder with a ruler or a scoring board tool will help you make scored creases in the paper and make crisp, sharply folded edges.

Generally, paper that is store-bought is cut precisely, thus making it much easier to fold. In the event that your accidently misalign the edges of the paper and have a lopsided folded card, you can square it up, using the cutting techniques on pages 25–26.

Folding with Fingers

1 With the paper positioned landscape, or horizontally in front of you, bend the paper to your left.

2 Align the corners of the paper and hold the edge together with your less dominant hand.

3 Slide your finger from the edge of the paper in a perpendicular direction to what will be the spine or fold.

4 Continue to slide your finger (or thumb) upward and then down again.

Mini Overbite

Aesthetically, it is a little more pleasing to overlap the edge of the card by 1 mm.

Folding with a Bone Folder and Ruler

1 Decide where you wish to place the fold, and draw a line using the bone folder and a ruler. Score the paper by pressing hard enough to indent the paper, but not so hard that you tear it.

2 Fold along scored line using the edge of the bone folder to press the paper, creating a nice crease.

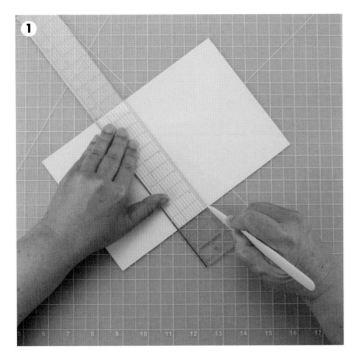

Using a Scoring Board Tool

There are a variety of tools available to create a precise score. The benefit of a scoring board tool is that scored lines tend to be straighter, because there is a premolded guide to create the scored lines. Sometimes, when using a bone folder and ruler, the ruler can slip. Scoring board tools have a secured thick edge on the board (called a stop) where you can align the paper, just like a guillotine or rotary cutting tool.

1 Align the paper and use the included folding tool to create the crease or scored lines for folding.

2 Scoring board tools tend to have guidelines that can help you decide where to place folded lines for more complicated folded cards.

Check Alignment

If the edges of the folded paper do not align properly, you can sometimes fix it. Hold the edges firmly (so they do not shift) and run the bone folder along the folded edge, adjusting the actual fold. Generally, this works for minor adjustments (less than 2 mm or 1/16 inch).

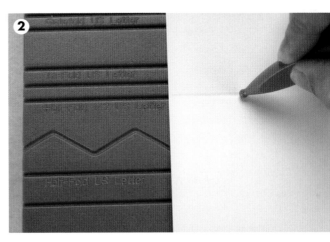

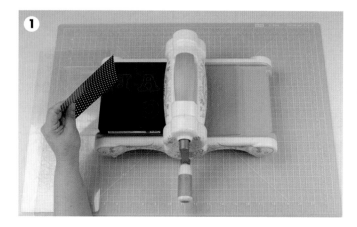

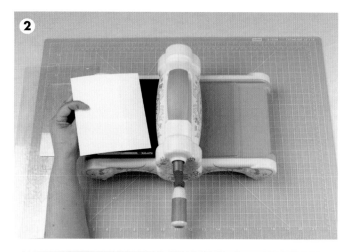

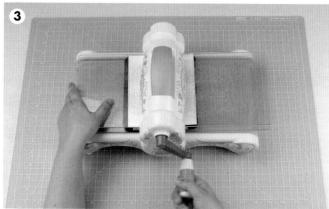

USING A DIE-CUTTING MACHINE

These machines come in a variety of shapes and sizes manufactured by different companies. Fortunately, many of the cutting dies and embossing folders can be used interchangeably. The key is the combination of shims (cutting plates) used to add the correct amount of pressure. This is how the dies either cut through the paper or only indent the paper. Like all machines, read the manufacturer's instructions.

Cutting with a Die-Cutting Machine

1 Make a "sandwich" by layering the correct order of cutting plate, cutting die, paper, and the second cutting plate.

2 For this die cut, place the paper printed side down on top of the cutting die.

3 Insert the sandwich into the opening of the machine and crank the handle in one direction.

4 Remove or strip the cut pieces from the sheet of paper and your die-cut images are ready to use.

Stripping the Pieces

Removing the little intricacies from detailed cutting dies can be tedious. Layer a sheet of wax paper between the paper and cutting die to help strip out the cut shape easily.

Embossing with a Die-Cutting Machine

With the same theory of the correct combination of shims (cutting plates) for different materials, follow the manufacturer's directions for embossing folders. Even aluminum cans can be embossed!

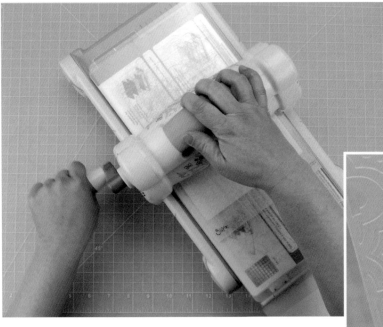

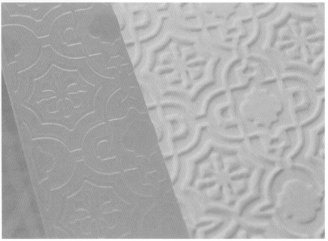

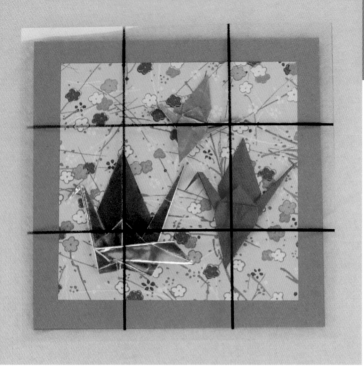

UNDERSTANDING COMPOSITION

The beauty of a handmade card is you control the look and feel of your work. One important, but not obvious, skill for making eye-popping and well-received cards is understanding composition. These are a few important elements that I borrowed from photography.

The Rule of Thirds

1 Divide your piece into thirds both horizontally and vertically (basically, draw an imaginary tic-tac-toe board over the entire area of your card).

2 Make the focus of the card along the lines or intersections of the lines.

"I will say right up front, however, that rules are meant to be broken and ignoring this one doesn't mean your images are necessarily unbalanced or uninteresting. However, a wise person once told me that if you intend to break a rule, you should always learn it first to make sure your breaking of it is all the more effective!"

—DARREN ROWSE

Odd Is Best—for Numbers, That Is

When composing a card, you can add as much stuff to it as you want. However, limiting the quantity to a small, odd number—one, three, or five—looks best. As with all of these "rules" they can be broken, but temporarily lay out the pieces and evaluate before you add the glue.

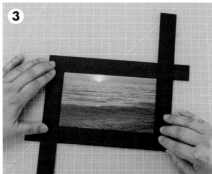

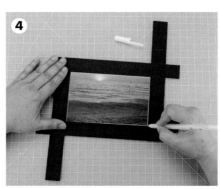

Many people see my stamped cards and ask, "How do you stamp an image straight and centered?" It's funny because I never thought about it. Early on, I would get very frustrated trying to stamp my images exactly where I wanted. I soon realized that if I just crop everything, I don't worry about stamping straight.

Cropping

My dad loves photography. He always looks at my photos and says, "The ocean is spilling. You can straighten it by cropping."

1 Assemble two 1 x 8-inch (2.5 x 20 cm) strips of paper into an "L" shape. It is important that this is square. Align on the gridlines printed on the cutting mat.

2 Using the guidelines on the cutting mat, position your photo (or artwork) so it is square. With one "L" shape in the upper-left corner, flip the second so the two are opposite each other.

3 Looking at the photo, position one "L" so the horizontal section is parallel with the horizon in the photo. The "L" guide will be at a funny angle. Bring the bottom "L" diagonally up and to the left, bringing the two "L" shapes closer together.

4 Mark the cutting lines and remove the "L" shapes so you can crop your photo.

1 Stamp the image.

2 Align the two "L" brackets to crop as explained at left.

3 Trace the cropped area and cut away.

Guidelines for Framing

Often, the focus of the card is a simple element in a frame. The guideline for framing is to add approximately 20 percent to the bottom margin with the sides and top margins equal. It is an optical illusion that helps make the composition of the card feel weighted and balanced. Sometimes, cards can feel top-heavy if the frame margins are equidistant on all four sides.

UNDERSTANDING AND USING COLOR

I find it interesting how color can affect people's moods. Choosing the colors to use when making cards is sometimes a challenge. I like to design my cards to reflect both my mood and the recipient's mood. Bright colors make me happy. However, deep colors can generate a richness for very special occasions. Cards without color or cards that are monochromatic (single color with variation in tone) have a dramatic impact and can express warmth with a very heartfelt message.

Color Wheel

I've found that a color wheel will sometimes help inspire ideas for a card. This tool is helpful when trying to decide which colors to use for an aesthetically pleasing project. A sampling of colors is organized and illustrates how primary colors can be blended to create secondary colors. Generally, this tool is the shape of a circle, with a second layer attached at a pivot point in the center of the circle. This layer has windows cut out that reveal contrasting or complementary color suggestions. Designers in different industries use the color wheel to help assemble pleasing color combinations for their creations.

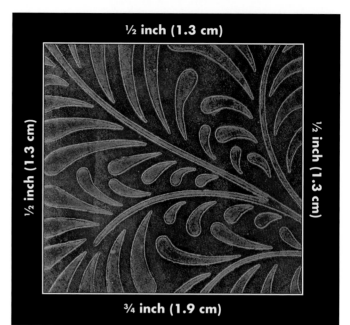

Complementary or Contrasting Colors

In elementary school, I remember learning about colors and how primary colors mixed together make secondary colors. Later, I learned about complementary colors. These colors, combined in the correct proportions, create white (not necessarily with pigments or ink but light) or black. They are also opposite or contrasting, which makes for dramatic or eye-popping cards. Using a variety of complementary colors, especially those combinations from a color wheel, will produce color schemes that are pleasing and can subtly convey the underlying mood for your cards.

Monochromatic

While it is fun to work with bright and complementary color combinations, sometimes the greatest impact is when there is no color or only shades or tints of one color. Ansel Adams and his stunning work with black-and-white photography is my inspiration for such cards. We can follow Ansel Adams's lead and use black-and-white photos to create beautiful cards.

CHOOSING PATTERNED PAPERS

Deciding which papers to use to make a card, might seem like an easy thing to do—especially after you've decided on the color scheme—but there are times when you experience "blank page dilemma." I've developed a method that gets me through these frozen moments. I look at what I'm wearing that day: teal, purple, and lime-colored blouse; khaki shorts; lime green sneakers.

Oh, and don't forget the green ponytail holder and gold earrings. Something about picking out your outfit is like picking out the pieces to make the card. Here is the card that was inspired based on the colors and patterns of my outfit.

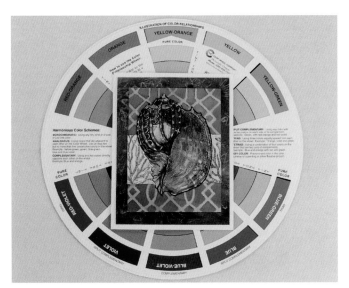

CARD STYLES AND METHODS

There are so many styles that can be used for cardmaking. Add to this the vast variety of embellishments, as well as textures of papers, and you can create cards for all ages, cultures, events—it's endless. Combine any of these with the basic skills of layout and color combinations and you will never be without a personalized, sincere greeting card that is perfect for any occasion.

Photo Cards

Capturing a moment in a photograph and sharing it is a great way to send a message. While electronically sending photos is wonderful, taking a little extra time to print your photo (whether it is printed by a photo service or by you) and turn it into a greeting card makes a real keepsake and a gift that is truly sincere.

FULL BLEED

You may have a photo that is virtually perfect and works "as is," but you still want to include a message. This style of photo card is easy and fast.

YOU WILL NEED

- 1 photo
- adhesive
- 1 sheet cream card stock, 8½ x 11 inches (21.6 x 28 cm)
- ruler
- bone folder
- paper trimmer

1 Adhere the photo to the bottom left corner of the card stock, making sure the left and bottom edges align.

2 Using a ruler and bone folder, score a horizontal line along the top of the photograph.

3 Fold the card.

4 Trim the excess card stock to the right and bottom of your photo.

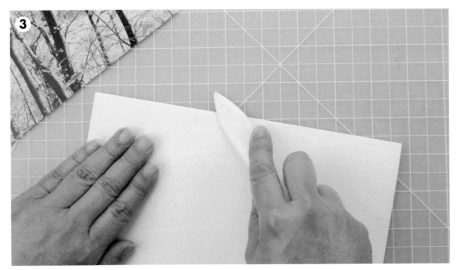

Use a Duplicate

Both conservationists and photographers would cringe with this step because applying glue directly to an original or professionally printed photo is not recommended. It is best to photocopy or duplicate the photo so the original remains unaltered.

YOU WILL NEED

- 1 sheet black card stock, 8½ x 11 inches (21.6 x 28 cm)
- 1 photo
- adhesive
- pencil
- ruler
- penknife
- cutting mat
- bone folder

FRAMED PHOTO

There are many ways to frame a photograph, but when it comes to turning your photograph into a greeting card, keeping it simple is often a priority.

Frame Like a Pro

Black or white photo mats are traditionally what professional photographers use to frame their prints. You can create a card that looks similar by choosing white or black card stock.

1. Orient the sheet of card stock vertically in front of you. With a pencil and ruler, draw horizontal and vertical guidelines ½ inch (1.3 cm) from the edges of the upper-left corner.

2. Align the upper-left corner of the photo along the right side of the left guideline and below the top guideline. The photo should now be ½ inch (1.3 cm) from the top and left edges of the card stock. Measure ½ inch (1.3 cm) to the right of the photo and draw the right guideline. Add the bottom guideline (which will be the fold) ½ inch (1.3 cm) from the bottom of the photo.

3. Trim the right side away with the ruler and penknife on a cutting mat.

4. Turn the card 90 degrees and score along the guideline that is ½ inch (1.3 cm) below the photo.

5. Apply adhesive to the photo, making sure it is spread as close to the edges of the photo as possible. Layer onto the front using the guidelines to keep the photo straight.

FRAMED PHOTO (PROFESSIONAL STYLE)

Professional photographers and conservationists prefer this style of framing photos. Note: This style of framed photo card will not alter the photo, so original photos are safe to use.

YOU WILL NEED

- 1 sheet white card stock, 15 x 7 inches (38 x 17.8 cm)
- 1 photo
- double-sided tape
- decorative card stock
- die-cut numbers
- ruler
- pencil
- bone folder or scoring tool
- penknife
- cutting mat
- marking pen in a color matching one color in the photo

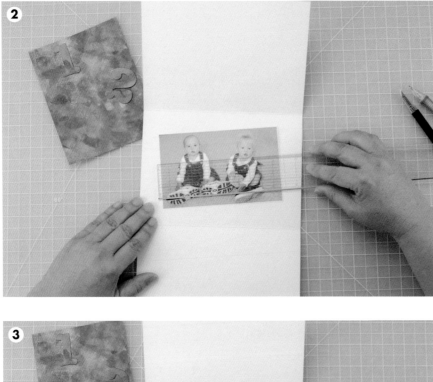

1 With the card stock aligned vertically in front of you, measure, mark, and score the card horizontally at the 5-inch and 10-inch (12.5 and 25 cm) marks.

2 To determine the size for the opening of the frame, measure the photo.

3 Subtract the length of the photo from the length of the card and divide by half. This gives you the side margin measurement. Repeat for the top and bottom margins. Draw guidelines with the pencil.

(continued)

Several Ways to Find the Center

Use the center-finding feature of grid-style rulers to determine the center of the card and establish the margins.

Thicker or Thinner Frames

You can adjust the frame width by increasing the margin size. There are occasions where a teeny photo in the middle of a large frame is very impressive.

4 Cut the guidelines with penknife and ruler on the cutting mat, creating the frame.

5 Apply a thin line of double-sided tape (¼ inch [6 mm]) to three sides of the frame as close to the outer edges as possible.

6 Fold over one panel and seal it to the frame along the three taped sides.

7 Insert the photo into the open side of the frame pocket.

8 To add color to the card frame, cut out a second smaller frame from decorative cardstock using the same method from step 4.

9 Adhere the die-cut "1" and "2" to the corners of the card. There is a little nursery rhyme that starts with "One, two, buckle my shoe." The boys in the photo are twins and they are wearing their daddy's shoes. The card would make everyone laugh if this nursery rhyme were written as the message inside the card.

10 Use the pen to write your message.

Change the Presentation

Whether you want the photo to be the focus of the card on the outside or the surprise on the inside depends on how the card panels are decorated. Cards can also be presented both vertically (portrait) or horizontally (landscape), depending on the direction of the layout.

YOU WILL NEED

- 1 photo
- double-sided tape
- 1 black folded note card, 1 inch (2.5 cm) longer and ½ inch (1.3 cm) taller than photo
- ruler
- calculator (optional)
- pencil
- paper trimmer

TRIPTYCH

Sometimes, a photo is nice but not quite perfect. This landscape photo of a rocky beach feels a little lonely, maybe empty. Cropping a photo makes you feel like you're looking at the scenery through a window.

1. Measure the length of the photo with the ruler and divide by three (you may need a calculator for this).

2. Using the ruler, mark these measurements on the back of the photo in pencil.

3. Using a paper trimmer, cut the photo vertically at the marks, making sure to keep the corners square.

4. Apply adhesive to each of the photo sections.

5. Layer the photo sections onto the folded note card. Starting with the left piece, align it at the ¼-inch (6 mm) margin on the left and centered vertically, with a ¼-inch (6 mm) margin top and bottom. Apply the second panel, leaving a ¼-inch (6 mm) margin at the left, top, and bottom edges. Repeat with the third panel.

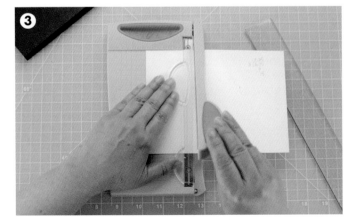

MINI FLOATING PHOTO

Surrounding a small photo with empty space is a very elegant presentation. For this card, the small photo is mounted to a Twinchie, which is a 2" (5 cm) square of heavy card stock or chipboard. You can purchase blank Twinchies, which are useful for all kinds of paper crafts, or simply cut your own square from a discarded cereal box or tablet cover.

YOU WILL NEED

- 4 strips card stock, 1 x 4 inches (2.5 x 10 cm)
- 1 Twinchie
- 1 photo
- adhesive
- 1 black folded note card, 5½ x 5½ inches (14 x 14 cm)
- 1 sheet white card stock, 5½ x 5½ inches (14 x 14 cm)
- paper clips
- bone folder
- penknife
- cutting mat
- ruler
- pencil

1 Create a cropping guide by using two of the 1 x 4-inch (2.5 x 10 cm) card stock strips to create an "L." Be sure to align the edges of the strips, making the "L" shape perpendicular. Repeat with the second pair of strips so there are now two "L" shapes. These will be your cropping guides.

2 To crop a photo to Twinchie size, place the Twinchie on your work surface in front of you. Lay one of the two "L" shapes on your work surface toward the bottom and left of the Twinchie. Lay the second "L" shape flipped 180 degrees and toward the upper-right side of the Twinchie. Push the two guides toward each other until they fit around the Twinchie.

3 Remove the Twinchie and use a couple of paper clips to secure the guides. Lay the guide over your photo, choosing the area you wish to keep.

4 Reapply the Twinchie to the middle of the cropping guide, and remove the cropping guide. Be sure the Twinchie does not move. Trace around the Twinchie with a bone folder.

5 Flip over the photo to see the scored lines on the back. This is where you will adhere the Twinchie. Apply adhesive to the photo and attach the Twinchie. Trim off the excess photo.

(continued)

6 Create a ½-inch (1.3 cm) frame on one of the panels of the black folded card stock by measuring and cutting a 4½-inch (11.4 cm) square.

7 Adhere the white sheet of card stock to the back panel of the card.

8 Adhere the Twinchie to the center of the white panel.

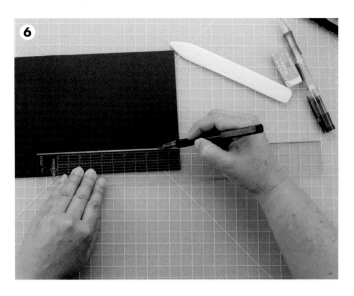

Make One Area Pop

Black-and-white photos can be stunning, but if you want to draw attention to one area of the photo, simply color in that area.

Collage

Derived from the French word *coller* ("to glue"), the word *collage* was coined to describe some of Pablo Picasso and Georges Braque's work. Both used collage to juxtapose their Cubist illustrations with realistic works. For a cardmaker, collage is great—so many wonderful things can be glued to the card, creating a meaningful message.

EPHEMERA

Ephemera are items that are supposed to be kept and used for a short time. Anything flat is perfect for cards. Tickets to events, postcards, information tags, and clips of relevant newspaper headlines create fun cards that send a message of fond memories, thinking of you, thank you for a great time, and more.

YOU WILL NEED

- 1 antique advertisement, such as a fishing creel
- 1 sheet cream card stock
- 1 ribbon with a width that fits the brass buckle and is approximately three-fourths the length of the card
- double-sided tape same width as ribbon
- 1 brass buckle
- 1 book page (from an old encyclopaedia, textbook, or dictionary) with text relating to ephemera object, 4 x 5½ inches (10 x 14 cm)
- 1 sheet marbled or patterned background paper in a matching color, 4¾ x 6¾ inches (12 x 17.2 cm)
- 1 piece ephemera, such as label from fishing lure box
- 1 cream-colored folded note card, 5 x 7 inches (12.5 x 17.8 cm)
- scissors
- pencil
- ruler
- 1 pair decorative-edged scissors (deckle edge)
- 1/16-inch (1.5 mm) hole punch

1. With scissors, crop the fishing creel advertisement so it has an ⅛-inch (3 mm) margin.

2. Layer onto the cream-colored card stock and draw an ⅛-inch (3 mm) guideline around it with a ruler.

3. Trim using deckled-edged scissors or a trimmer and set aside.

4. Apply the double-sided tape to one side of the ribbon, leaving the tape's release backing intact. Trim one end of the ribbon to a point with the scissors.

5. Punch a 1/16-inch (1.5 mm) hole approximately halfway along the ribbon.

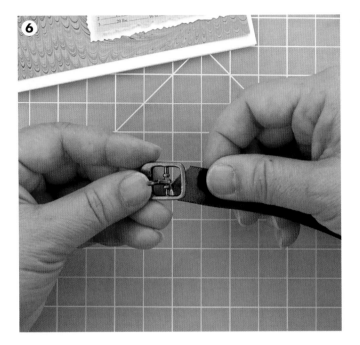

6 Slide the buckle onto the ribbon. Insert the prong of the buckle into the hole to secure.

7 To assemble the card, layer the book page on the marbled paper. Adhere the fishing creel advertisement to the card in the bottom-right corner. Peel off the release liner from the ribbon and adhere to the card approximately 1½ inches (3.8 cm) from the left of the card, leaving 1 inch (2.5 cm) of overlap on the top of the marbled paper. Fold the ribbon over the top of this layer and adhere to the back. Add the fishing-lure label approximately halfway down the piece on top of the buckled ribbon and to the left side approximately ½ inch (1.3 cm) from the edge. Layer the entire collage onto the folded note card, leaving an ⅛-inch (3 mm) margin.

YOU WILL NEED

- 1 textbook page, 6 x 6 inches (15 x 15 cm)

- ink pads in brown, dark brown, and black

- gold and white paint

- adhesive

- 1 olive-green folded note card, 5½ x 5½ inches (14 x 14 cm)

- 3 gold star brad embellishments

- 1 sheet decorative paper with gold highlights in burgundy and mauve, 5½ x ¾ inch (14 x 2 cm)

- rubber stamp of large bee

- pencil

- ruler

- long-handled lighter

- penknife (optional)

- cutting mat (if using penknife)

- stenciling-style paintbrush

- black pigment ink pad

- clear embossing powder

- embossing heat tool or heat source

ALTERED TEXTBOOK PAGE

Sometimes, old textbook pages make great background paper. You can use the topic of the page as the theme of your card. People really do read the text in the background, so it makes this card interesting and clever.

Note: Alternatively, create a faux burned edge by using the penknife to cut a loose, wavy line along the guideline. Apply brown ink approximately ¼ inch (6 mm) from the edge with the ink pad. Continue with dark brown and black inks, graduating each color toward the edge.

1 Stamp the textbook page with the bee in black ink.

2 To create antiqued edges for the textbook page, draw a ½-inch (1.3 cm) guideline in pencil around the perimeter using a ruler. Burn one edge of the paper with the lighter. Keep your eye on the guideline and blow out the flame approximately ¼ inch (6 mm) from the pencil mark. Continue around the textbook page to burn all the edges.

3 Color the bee using gold ink for the bee's body and white for the wings.

4 Adhere the textbook page to the folded note card.

5 Add the gold star brads to the left side of the burgundy strip, starting at ¾ inch (2 cm) and leaving ⅛ inch (3 mm) between brads. Adhere the strip to the upper one-third of the card.

YOU WILL NEED

- 3 magazine pages predominately monochromatic in different color schemes
- water-based glaze
- 1 sheet decorative card stock in shades of baby blue, 8 ⅜ x 3 ½ inches (21.4 x 9 cm)
- adhesive
- 1 navy blue folded note card, 8 ⅝ x 3 ¾ inches (22 x 9.5 cm)
- 3–5 round hole punches in graduating diameters
- broad paintbrush
- paper trimmer

Decoupage (a variation of collage)

Here's an interesting craft where cutout printed papers are glued to flat surfaces to achieve the appearance of detailed, painted, or decorated façades. This technique started centuries ago to reproduce works of art on panels of cabinets, tables, cupboards, serving trays, and much more. Often, duplicate layers of the focus image were cut out and glued with lacquers. The final piece used multiple layers of the clear lacquer, which ultimately filled in the spaces to one level. This created a dimensional illusion of depth. Today, water-based glazes and foam tape add a modern interpretation, making this technique easy and impressive for cardmaking.

PUNCHED MAGAZINE PAGES

Turn magazines and other printed materials into fun greeting cards with a little glue, a pair of scissors, and an eye for texture and color.

1 Using the second to the largest diameter circle, punch out several pieces from different magazine pages.

2 Using the largest diameter circle, position the punch over the previously punched circle. This will create a circle with a hole.

3 Continue punching holes and circles in different sizes and with different openings.

4 With a paintbrush, apply a generous amount of water-based glaze to the decorative card stock. For this size of paper, use a pool of glaze about 1 inch (2.5 cm) in diameter and spread with a broad paintbrush. Lay the punched circles in the glaze and continue applying the glaze. Make sure there are no air bubbles under the applied circles.

Hang Over the Edges

Apply circles so they hang off the edges of the card. Once the glaze is dry, trim the circles so they are flush. This makes the piece aesthetically pleasing.

5 Apply two or three coats of glaze, making sure each layer is dry before applying the next coating of glaze.

6 Crop overhanging pieces with a paper trimmer.

7 Adhere the dried piece to the folded notecard.

YOU WILL NEED

- magazine pages with predominant colors of red, dark brown, and pink
- adhesive
- 1 white folded note card, 5 x 7 inches (12.5 x 17.8 cm)
- water-based glaze
- pencil
- scissors
- broad paintbrush
- penknife (optional)
- cutting mat (if using penknife)

FREEFORM CUTTING

Create visual depth with a truly personal touch. Cut simple figures and shapes from colorful magazine pages and apply them to the card front in a layered decoupage. You can find many ways to recycle magazine pages for cardmaking.

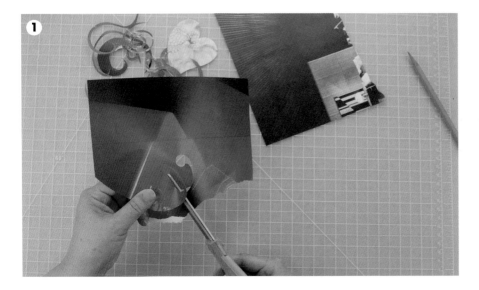

1. With a pencil, draw squiggly lines and curves on the back of the magazine page and cut out with scissors. Then, cut out a heart.
   Optional: Use the penknife and cutting mat instead of scissors to cut out the swirls.

2. Crop a dark brown magazine page to 4¾ x 6¾ inches (12 x 17 cm) and adhere to the folded card.

3. With a paintbrush, apply water-based glaze to the entire surface of the dark brown layer. Add the cutout swirls and the heart to the wet glaze. Let dry. Apply a second layer of glaze over the entire surface of the card. Let dry.

ETCHED FLORAL TRIO

Here's a modern method for creating decoupage dimension.

YOU WILL NEED

- water-based glaze
- 3 copies printed floral trio
- 1 sheet scarlet card stock, 5 x 3 inches (12.5 x 7.5 cm)
- 1 houndstooth-pattern folded note card, 5 x 7 inches (12.5 x 17.8 cm)
- adhesive
- double-sided adhesive foam squares
- paintbrush
- scissors

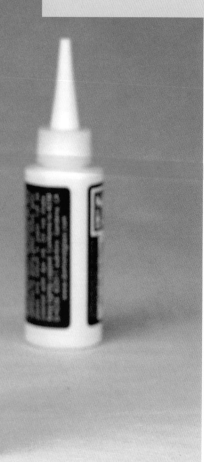

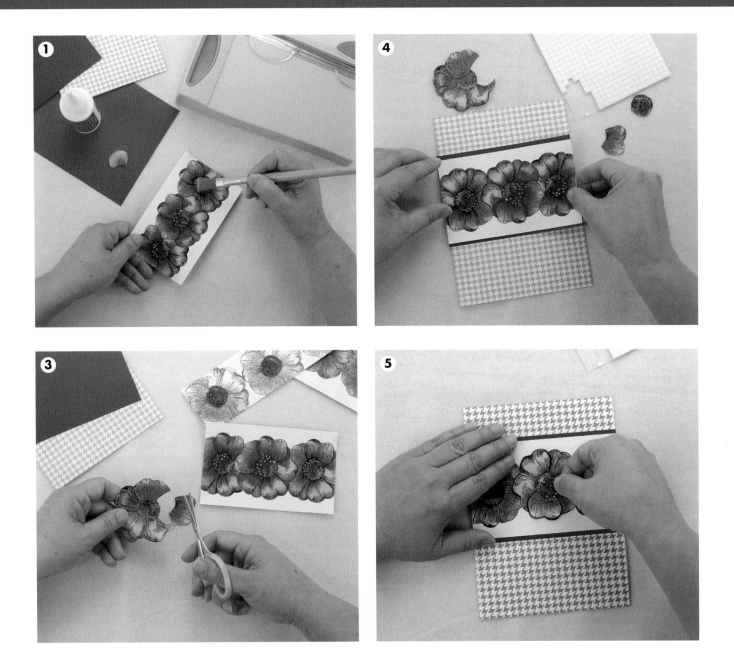

1 With a paintbrush, apply the glaze to all three copies of the floral trio. Let dry.

2 With scissors, crop one copy to 5 x 2¾ inches (12.5 x 7 cm). This will be your base layer.

3 Cut out the center disk of the flower from the second copy. Set aside. Cut out the center flower from the third copy and cut one petal off. Cut slits along the side edges of the remaining petals up to the center disk of the flower. Slightly curl under the sides of the petals with your fingers.

4 Adhere the base layer onto the scarlet card stock and adhere to the folded card.

5 Align the cutout flower with the base layer and adhere the center of the flower with double-sided foam squares. This will elevate the second layer, giving the flower depth. Apply the cutout floral disk to the center flower with foam squares.

YOU WILL NEED

- double-sided adhesive tape

- 1 sheet decorative marbled paper, 3 x 5½ inches (7.5 x 14 cm)

- 1 sheet decorative paper colored with walnut ink, 4 x 5¼ inches (10 x 13.3 cm)

- 1 strip decorative cream-colored paper, 1 x 5½ inches (2.5 x 14 cm)

- beeswax

- 3 pen nibs and trinket charms

- 1 kraft-colored folded note card, 4¼ x 5½ inches (10.8 x 14 cm)

- heat tool

COLLAGE WITH WAX

Beeswax was used as an adhesive centuries ago. Alone, it is a low-tack method to glue things together, but added to pine resin it is much more effective. But for a cardmaker's purpose, beeswax alone adds an ambience of nostalgia and a vintage feel. Working with melted beeswax can be dangerous, as it is hot. Use with caution.

1 Because beeswax will resist tapes and glues, it is best to apply double-sided adhesive tape to the back of the marbled paper, walnut ink–stained paper, and cream-colored strip as your first step.

2 Adhere the cream-colored strip to the marbled paper. Adhere the marbled paper to the ink-stained paper, and the ink-stained paper to the card.

3 With a heat tool, melt the beeswax over the strip. It's okay if the beeswax spreads beyond the strip.

4 Place the trinkets and pen nibs onto the melted wax along the paper strip. Remelt the wax with the heat tool if it has cooled and solidified.

5 Let cool before lifting or the trinkets will slide off.

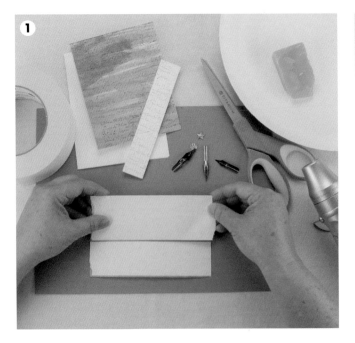

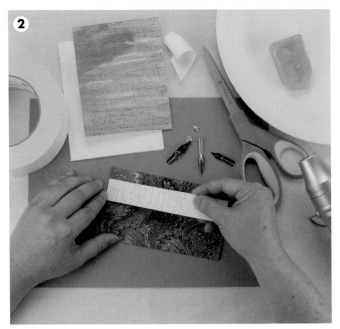

Embellishments

Dimension and texture make your greeting cards interesting and fun. Just about anything that is flat (up to ¼ inch [6 mm]) and fits on a card can embellish and personalize your handmade greetings. From crystal beads to satin ribbons, anything looks great on a card.

CLEAR MICRO BEADS

Micro glass beads are a beautiful addition to your cards. Mostly made from crystal glass, they capture the light and bring a twinkle with an air of elegance.

YOU WILL NEED

- clear glaze adhesive
- 1 sheet decorative card stock, 4¼ x 5½ inches (10.8 x 14 cm)
- clear glass "micro" beads
- 1 white folded note card, 5 x 7 inches (12.5 x 17.8 cm)
- charm or trinket
- ½-inch (1.3 cm)-hwide ribbon, 10 inches (25.4 cm)
- paintbrush

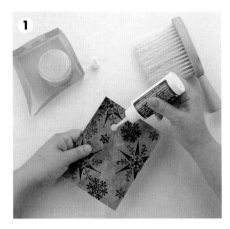

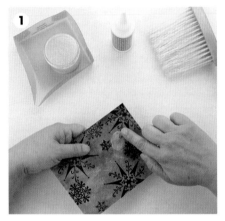

1 Evenly apply a ¾-inch (2 cm) diameter of clear glaze adhesive to the decorative card stock. You can use a broad paintbrush or your finger. Water-based glaze adhesive will clean up easily. Check with the manufacturer as each type of glaze may differ.

2 Pour the glass beads over the glazed surface of the card stock. Use a tray to capture the beads so you can return unused beads to the container. Let dry.

3 Adhere the beaded card stock to the folded card.

4 Tie the charm or trinket to the ribbon and glue the ribbon to the front of the card. Wrap the left end to the back of the card and the right end to the back of the front panel.

Fingers Are Sensitive

I like using my finger for this style of adhesive application. Fingers are easily cleaned and always at hand!

Even Distribution

Knowing how much adhesive to use to adhere these glass beads might not seem important, but it is. Too much adhesive and the distribution of beads becomes lumpy; not enough adhesive will leave open spots. Using half the diameter of the bead for the depth of the glue will result in an even distribution of beads.

YOU WILL NEED

- clear glaze adhesive
- 1 sheet deep red card stock stamped with swirls, 2 x 5½ inches (5 x 14 cm)
- gold micro beads
- 1 sheet striped printed card stock, 3 x 5½ inches (7.5 x 14 cm)
- 1 kraft-colored folded note card, 4¼ x 5½ inches (10.8 x 14 cm)

FREEHAND SWIRLS AND GOLD BEADS

Using a rubber-stamped image as a guide, add a swirl to your card with gold glass beads for a luxurious appearance.

1. With the fine tip of the adhesive bottle, trace around the swirl design on the red card stock. It is okay not to follow the pattern exactly.

2. Pour the gold glass beads over the wet adhesive. Let loose beads fall into a tray and return unused glass beads to the container. Let dry.

3. Adhere to the striped card stock and then adhere to the folded card.

Household Found Objects

There are so many things that can be added to a card that are beyond the object's usual scope of use. A little glue + some imagination = fun and whimsical messages.

BUTTONS AS MUSIC

This is the perfect card for the musician in your life. Turn colorful buttons into music notes and you're sure to generate a smile.

1. Starting with the white card stock, stamp the treble clef image onto the left side of the card, about 1 inch (2.5 cm) from the left edge.

2. Using the ruler and black pen, draw one horizontal line starting ½ inch (1.3 cm) from the left edge and intersecting near the end of the curl in the center of the treble clef. This will be the G line in the staff of music. Stop ½ inch (1.3 cm) from the right edge of the paper.

3. Measure ⅜ inch (1 cm) below the horizontal line and draw a parallel line, matching both ends of the previously drawn line. This will be the E line.

4. Draw three additional lines moving upward from the G line. You should now have five horizontal lines and this is now your music staff.

5. Rubber stamp the numbers "3" and "4" just to the right of the treble clef.

6. Using the sheet music as a guide, draw two vertical lines to create the measures.

7. Glue the buttons onto the music lines as indicated by the sheet music.

8. Draw ascenders and descenders for the music notes.

9. Crop so the treble clef has ¼-inch (6 mm) top and bottom margins. Make sure you crop the card so the music staff is straight. Adhere the layer to the folded card stock.

BAND-AIDS

Sending a unique message to someone who has the sniffles or an injury is sure to bring a comforting smile. These little adhesive bandages send a whimsical, yet heartfelt, message.

YOU WILL NEED

- 1 medium adhesive bandage
- 2 mini adhesive bandages
- 1 sheet white card stock, 2¼ x 3½ inches (5.7 x 8.9 cm)
- adhesive
- 3 pairs googly eyes
- 1 sheet decorative cardstock, 4 x 5¼ inches (10 x 13.3 cm)
- 1 mustard folded note card, 4½ x 5½ inches (11.4 x 14 cm)
- die-cut "thought cloud"
- black medium-point marker
- pen
- wax pencil for lifting small objects

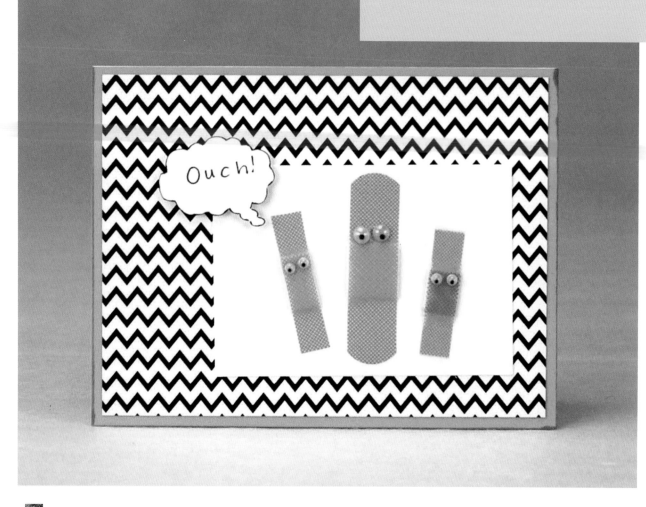

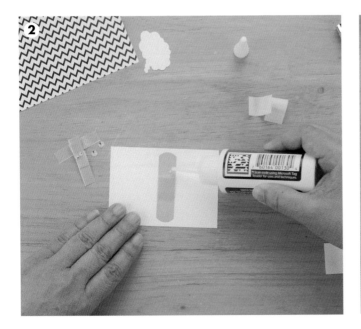

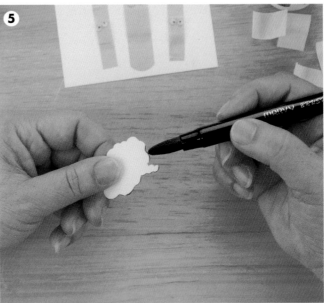

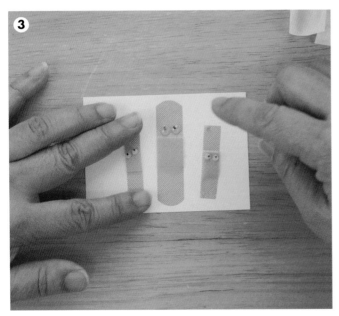

1 Peel off the protective paper on the medium-size adhesive bandage to reveal the adhesive. Apply to the center of the smaller piece of white card stock.

2 Apply two small drops of glue to the adhesive bandage and adhere the googly eyes. Use the wax pencil to lift and position the eyes.

3 Repeat with the mini adhesive bandages on either side of the medium adhesive bandage.

4 Adhere to the decorative card stock and then to the folded note card.

5 Color the edge of the "thought cloud" with a black marker. This adds an outline to the cloud, making it stand out on the card. Adhere to the card.

6 Write your sentiment in the cloud. Depending on how big your thought cloud is, the message can be as sympathetic as "Ouch" or "Hope you are feeling better soon."

YOU WILL NEED

- 1 paper napkin
- paper adhesive
- 1 sheet cream card stock, 8½ x 5½ inches (21.6 x 14 cm)
- 1 strip decorative card stock, 1¼ x 4 inches (3.2 x 10 cm)
- 1 charm
- ¼-inch (6 mm)-wide satin ribbon, 12 inches (30.5 cm)
- 1 light blue folded note card, 3¾ x 8⅝ inches (9.5 x 22 cm)
- scissors
- broad paintbrush
- paper trimmer

NAPKIN ART

Beautifully printed paper napkins are little works of art and are often too pretty to casually throw away. The art of decoupage inspired this clever use on greeting cards. Take an inexpensive napkin and turn it into a very special card.

How to Unstick the Stuck

Use two pieces of a light adhesive masking tape (painter's tape) to pull apart the napkin layers. Tip from Susan Pickering Rothamel.

1 Separate or peel apart the layers of the printed napkin.

2 Cut away the excess napkin.

3 Apply paper adhesive to the cream-colored card stock and spread with a broad paintbrush.

4 Lay the printed napkin onto the wet adhesive and gently press using the paintbrush. The edges of the napkin should disappear. Let the paper dry, but clean your brush before the adhesive dries on the brush.

5 Crop to 3¼ x 5 inches (8.3 x 12.5 cm).

6 Adhere the decorative card stock strip on top. Tie on the charm by wrapping the ribbon around the napkin-decorated piece. Adhere to the folded card, securing the ribbon.

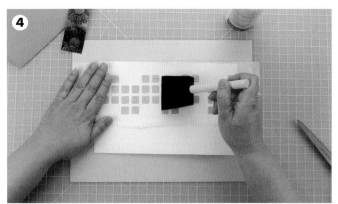

CUTOUT NAPKIN

The printed patterns on napkins are varied and when the pattern does not fit on your card, you can make it fit. Just cut out the images.

YOU WILL NEED

- 1 paper napkin
- paper adhesive
- 1 sheet cream card stock, 4¼ x 5½ inches (10.8 x 14 cm)
- 1 peach-colored folded note card, 4¼ x 5½ inches (10.8 x 14 cm)
- baker's twine
- scissors
- paintbrush

1 Separate the printed layer of the napkin. Choose the images you wish to use for your card and cut them out.

2 Using the paper adhesive, apply the napkin cutouts to the cream-colored card stock. Because the adhesive dries clear, you can apply adhesive to the card stock and lay the delicate napkin layer on the wet adhesive. You can also smooth out wrinkles with more paper adhesive and a paintbrush. Let the paper dry, but clean your paintbrush before the adhesive dries.

3 Crop to 4¼ x 4¾ inches (10.8 x 12 cm) and adhere to the folded card. Tie baker's twine and secure with a bow.

YOU WILL NEED

- 1 elegantly printed napkin
- paper adhesive
- 1 sheet cream card stock,
  5½ x 4¼ inches (14 x 10.8 cm)
- 1¾-inch (4.4 cm)-wide grosgrain ribbon,
  15 inches (38 cm)
- 1 sheet yellow card stock,
  5½ x 4¼ inches (14 x 10.8 cm)
- 1 plum-colored folded note card,
  5½ x 5½ inches (14 x 14 cm)
- broad paintbrush
- scissors
- paper trimmer

SOPHISTICATED SERVIETTE

These elegant napkins are too pretty to wipe your mouth after biting into a juicy hamburger. So save one and make a fabulous card.

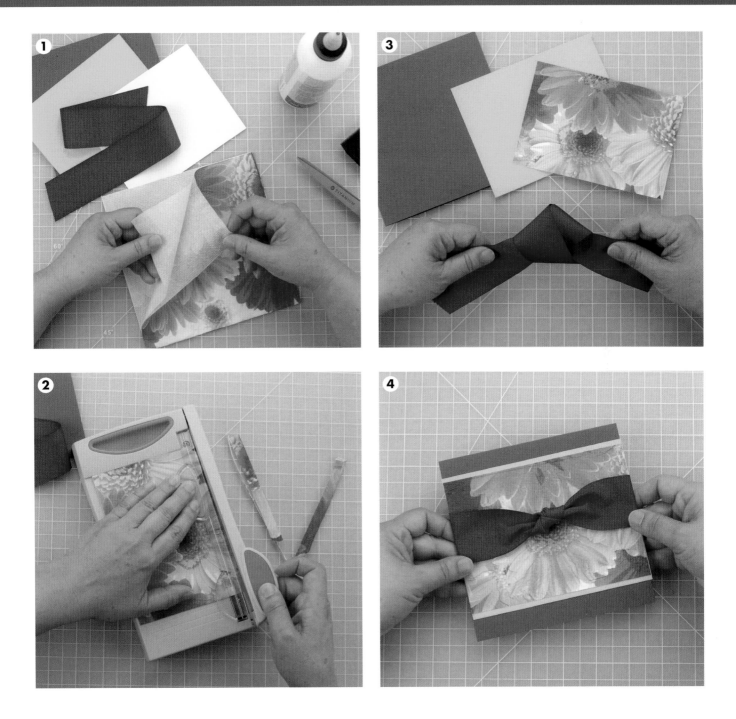

1 Separate the printed layer of the napkin. Cut out the part you wish to use.

2 Apply paper adhesive to the cream-colored card stock and press the printed napkin layer onto the wet adhesive. Gently push any air bubbles to the edge of the card. Let dry. Trim to 4¾ x 5½ inches (12 x 14 cm).

3 Tie a single knot in the middle of the ribbon.

4 Adhere the napkin to yellow card stock. Adhere the ribbon, wrapping the ends and securing them to the back of the yellow card. Adhere everything on the folded card.

PAPER CUPCAKE LINERS

Everyone loves cupcakes, those little cakes originally baked in cups. With the invention of paper cupcake liners after World War II, bakers could be sure their little cakes would release out of the baking cups. The cupcake liner also helped keep fingers sticky-free while maintaining moisture and freshness. Cupcake liners are now made in different sizes and printed in a variety of colors, patterns, and finishes, but they also make great additions for clever and happy greeting cards.

YOU WILL NEED

- 5 mini cupcake liners in different colors or patterns, with at least one in green (for the leaves)
- 3 adhesive-backed pearls
- ⅛-inch (3 mm)-wide olive green satin ribbon, 12 inches (30.5 cm)
- 1 yellow folded note card, 8⅝ x 3¾ inches (22 x 9.5 cm)
- double-sided tape
- adhesive
- scissors
- yellow permanent marker

1. Start with one cupcake liner and fold it in half. Repeat to fold it in quarters and finally into eighths.

2. With scissors, trim the open end of the folded cupcake liner into an arch. Open and, if needed, pinch the center to create a more floral-looking shape. Continue with the remaining liners, leaving the green liner for the next step.

3. Cut the green cupcake liner into four pie-shaped pieces. Using one of the quarters, pinch the narrow end into a point. Gather the full end to a point and flatten. This will make a leaf shape.

4. To change the color of the self-adhesive pearl, use a permanent marker to color the white pearl golden yellow.

5. Assemble the flowers by adhering three strips of the green satin ribbon onto the folded card. For best results, use double-sided tape.

6. Adhere the flowers, pearls, and leaves to finish your card.

YOU WILL NEED

- 1 doily, 4 inches (10 cm) diameter
- dimensional fabric paint (pearl)
- ⅛-inch (3 mm)-wide white satin ribbon, 3 inches (7.5 cm)
- adhesive
- 1 eggplant-colored folded note card, 8⅝ x 3¾ inches (22 x 9.5 cm)
- 1 sheet decorative card stock in mauve color to complement note card color, 3¼ x 5 inches (8.3 x 12.5 cm)
- pencil
- ruler
- scissors

DOILY SUNDRESS

Handmade, decorative wool adornments used in the eighteenth century were made popular by the Doily family, who created delicate and intricate lacy patterns and shapes. These little fabric objects were often used as the napkin accompanying a finger bowl or to show off a beautifully presented dish. With the invention of the printing press and the abundance of paper products, paper doilies were widely used instead of the more valuable and irreplaceable crochet and tatted doilies. Because doilies give the impression of elegance and femininity, they make a great addition to cards for the women in your life.

1 Doilies generally have patterned scalloped edges. These patterns tend to repeat 180 degrees. Use one of the unique scallops as the center of the bodice on the doily dress and the center of the bottom hem of the dress.

2 On the back of the doily, using a ruler, draw a guideline from the indentation of the scallop to the beginning of the nonembossed area of the doily. Continue this line at a slight angle to the bottom edge, completing the guideline at the top of the curve on the scallop. Repeat this guideline as a mirror image of the first line.

3 Cut the guidelines with scissors.

4 On the front of the doily, apply three small drops of dimensional fabric paint to create three little pearls. Let dry.

5 Tie the ends of the ribbon together in a knot. Adhere the loop to the back of the doily dress at the neckline.

6 Adhere the doily dress to the decorative card stock and layer onto the folded card stock.

7 Just above to the left and below to the right of the decorative card stock layer, apply three more little pearls with the dimensional fabric paint. Let dry.

SILK DAISY FLOWERS

Artificial flowers have been enjoyed for ages, but the relatively recent invention of silk flowers changed how a cardmaker can use these flexible fabric flowers in paper crafts.

YOU WILL NEED

- 1 silk daisy
- fabric adhesive
- 1 sheet gingham card stock, 5¼ x 4 inches (13.4 x 10 cm)
- 1 white folded note card, 5½ x 4¼ inches (14 x 10.8 cm)
- olive-colored rickrack trimming, 5½ inches (14 cm)
- 1 gold-colored button
- piece metallic cording, 3 inches (7.5 cm)
- scissors

1 Remove the silk daisy from the plastic stem by cutting the plastic stamen from the stem. This will separate the flower petals so they can be applied flat.

2 Glue the petals together with adhesive. Set aside.

3 Adhere the gingham card stock to the folded card stock with an ⅛-inch (3 mm) margin.

4 Adhere the rickrack trimming horizontally to the gingham layer approximately 1½ inches (3.8 cm) from the bottom of the card.

5 Glue the daisy to the card on top of the rickrack.

6 Tie a knot on top of the button using the cord. Trim the ends.

7 Adhere the button in the center of the daisy petals.

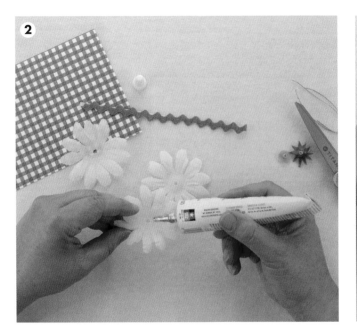

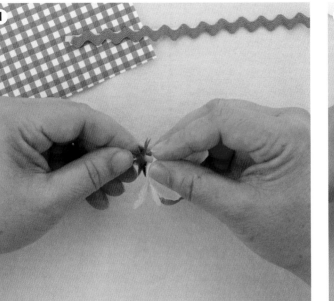

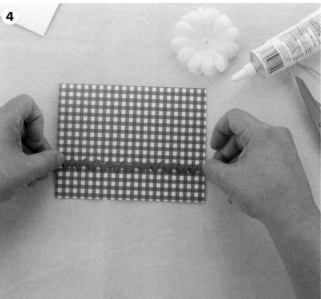

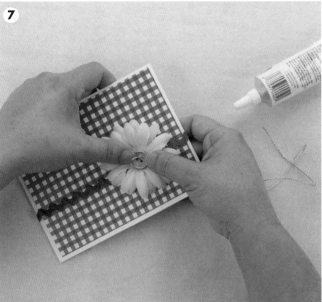

YOU WILL NEED

- 1 silk flower with leaves
- fabric adhesive
- 3 rhinestones, 2 mm
- gold mizuhiki paper cord, 10 inches (25.4 cm)
- ⅛-inch (3 mm)-wide gold ribbon, 30 inches (76 cm)
- 1 sheet gold decorative card stock, 4 x 5¼ inches (10 x 13.3 cm)
- 1 white folded note card, measuring 4¼ x 5½ inches (10.8 x 14 cm)
- scissors
- gold metallic marker

GOLDEN SILK LEAVES

A metallic marker transforms these silk leaves into an impressive golden card.

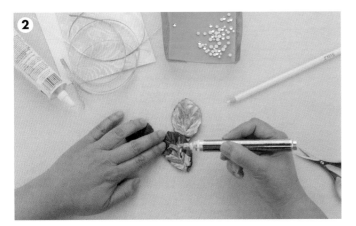

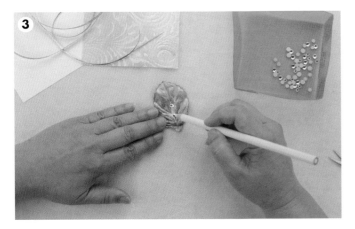

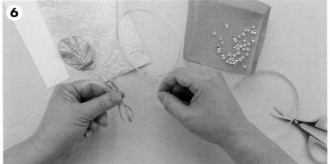

1 Cut the leaves off the silk flower branch.

2 Using a metallic marker, color one side of three leaves. Let dry. Color the back of each leaf.

3 Adhere the three rhinestones to one silk leaf.

4 Create stems for the leaves by adhering a 2-inch (5 cm) length of mizuhiki paper cord to the back of each leaf.

5 Wrap the ribbon lengthwise two times around the left third of the gold-colored card stock, creating two parallel lines. Secure the ends of the ribbon to the back of the card stock.

6 Create a double bow by wrapping ribbon around three fingers two times and tie in the center with a smaller piece of ribbon.

7 Glue the three leaves to the card stock over the parallel ribbon and adhere to the folded card, leaving an ⅛-inch (3 mm) frame.

Natural Objects and Materials

Dried leaves from a walk on a brisk autumn day, sprigs of aromatic lavender from the garden, that ancient bag of dried bean soup that you found in the back of the cupboard: all things that can be turned into a greeting card with a little glue, a piece of card stock, and a little imagination.

LENTILS MAKE THE OWL

YOU WILL NEED

- black ink pad
- 1 sheet kraft-colored decorative card stock, 3¾ x 5 inches (9.4 x 12.5 cm)
- water-based adhesive that dries clear
- legumes and grains: red and green lentils, split peas, white beans, black-eyed peas, wild rice, popcorn
- double-sided tape
- 1 sheet green card stock, 4 x 5¼ inches (10 x 13.3 cm)
- 1 eggplant-colored folded note card, 4¼ x 5½ inches (10.8 x 14 cm)
- rubber stamp of owl or outline print out of owl
- bamboo skewer (to apply glue)

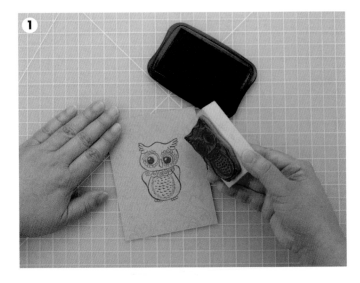

1 Rubber stamp the owl onto the kraft-colored card stock.

2 Use the bamboo skewer to apply glue to the owl image.

3 Adhere the different colored lentils, peas, and beans in places that resemble the colors of an owl. Let dry.

4 With double-sided tape, adhere the finished owl image to the green card stock and then adhere to the folded card.

YOU WILL NEED

- 1 die-cut scalloped oval shape
- 1 decorative folded note card,
  4¼ x 5½ inches (10.8 x 14 cm)
- double-sided tape
- adhesive
- pressed dried flowers

PRESSED DRIED FLOWERS

A keepsake from a special event or the reward from a beautifully planted garden: a pressed flower can be preserved, but more important, it can be sent as the keepsake for that special celebration.

1 Adhere the oval shape to the folded card with double-sided tape.

2 Adhere the dried flowers to the die-cut oval.

PRESSED DRIED LEAVES

Crisp and wildly colorful, autumn leaves are inspiration for warm and heartfelt messages. Although you can use printed papers or prefabricated embellishments, a sustainable source is provided by nature.

YOU WILL NEED

- adhesive
- 3 pressed leaves in graduating sizes and colors
- 1 sheet kraft-colored card stock, 4 x 5¼ inches (10 x 13.3 cm)
- 1 sheet burgundy card stock, 4¼ x 5½ inches (10.8 x 14 cm)
- double-sided tape
- kraft-colored paper ribbon, 18 inches (45.7 cm)
- 1 kraft-colored folded note card, 5 x 7 inches (12.5 x 17.8 cm)
- scissors

1 Adhere the pressed leaves to the kraft-colored card stock and let dry.

2 Adhere to the burgundy-colored card stock with double-sided tape.

3 Wrap the paper ribbon around both layers approximately 1 inch (2.5 cm) from the bottom. Tie a square knot. Trim the ends.

4 Adhere to the folded card with the top and sides equidistant and the bottom margin a little larger.

Ribbons and String

To me, ribbon means gifts and packages. Maybe it makes me think there's an element of surprise and delight. Receiving a card decorated with a ribbon always brings a smile. The message is subtle but has high impact.

SIMPLE PACKAGE

Sometimes, a card's elegance lies in the simplicity of its components: a square piece of paper, a ribbon, and a bow.

YOU WILL NEED

- double-sided tape
- 2 pieces satin ribbon, 4 inches (10 cm) and 7 inches (17.8 cm)
- 1 sheet decorative card stock, 2¾ x 2¾ inches (7 x 7 cm)
- 1 white folded note card, 3¾ x 8⅝ inches (9.5 x 22 cm)
- adhesive

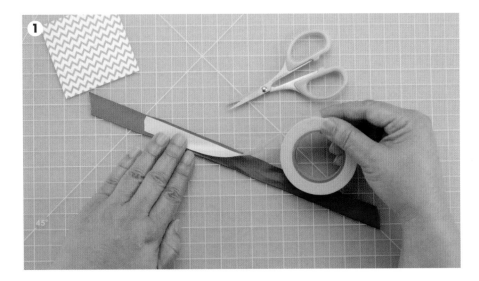

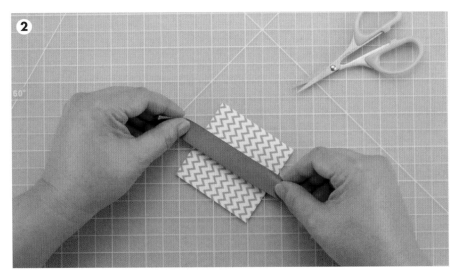

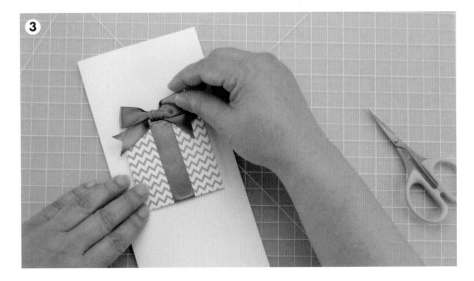

1 Apply double-sided tape to the back of the 4-inch (10 cm) length of ribbon.

2 Adhere vertically to the decorative sheet of card stock. Wrap the ends to the back of the card stock and secure.

3 Adhere this square to the folded card. Tie a bow with the second piece of ribbon and glue to the top of the square, creating the image of a packaged gift.

ELEGANT BOW

A little swirl adds movement and a few rhinestones add sparkle—
simply elegant.

YOU WILL NEED

- black ink pad
- 1 white folded note card,
  5 x 7 inches
  (12.5 x 17.8 cm)
- 1 velvet ribbon, 18 inches
  (45.7 cm)
- glue
- 3 rhinestones, 2 mm
- scissors
- rubber stamp of swirl
- pencil
- ruler
- $\frac{1}{16}$-inch (1.5 mm) hole punch
- penknife
- cutting mat

1. Rubber stamp the swirl image on the upper-left and lower-right corners on the front of the folded card. Measure and mark two holes along the fold approximately 3 inches (7.5 cm) from the top and ¾ inch (2 cm) apart. Punch out.

2. Slice open the space between the holes with the penknife on a cutting mat.

3. Thread the ribbon through the slit and tie a bow on the front.

4. Adhere the three rhinestones on the left side of the bow.

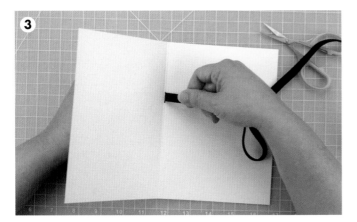

Picking Up Rhinestones Made Easy

A soft marking pencil picks up rhinestones or other hard-to-hold embellishments, making gluing much easier.

YOU WILL NEED

- 1 piece burlap, 4¼ x 1½ inches (10.8 x 3.8 cm)
- 1 sheet decorative card stock, 4¼ x 3 inches (10.8 x 7.5 cm)
- double-sided tape
- 1 satin ribbon, 14 inches (35.6 cm)
- 1 kraft-colored folded note card, 4¼ x 5½ inches (10.8 x 14 cm)
- glue
- 1 gold-colored bird (swallow) charm
- scissors

SIMPLE GRANNY KNOT

Watercrafts were part of our lives and learning how to tie knots an important part of working with boats. How to tie a reef (or square) knot was easy to remember because there was a little rhyme: "Right over left, left over right, makes this knot both tidy and tight." However, a granny knot is sometimes the outcome when learning how to tie the square knot. It is the result of "right over left," and again "right over left." Not as secure as the square knot but perfectly appealing for cardmaking.

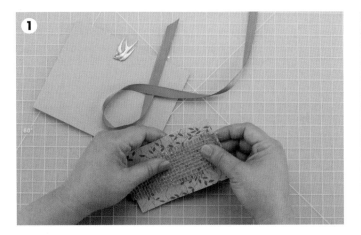

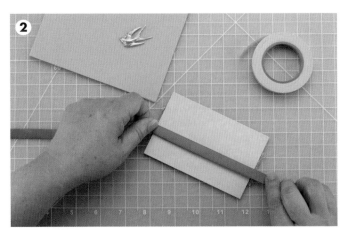

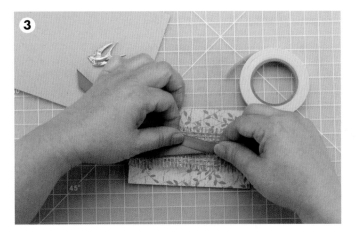

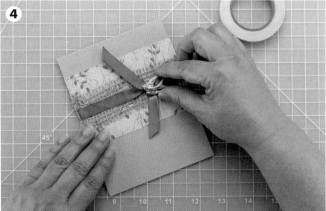

Wrap Around and Around

There are times when ribbon can be used as a closure for your card. To do this, secure the ribbon on the back of the card, wrap it around to the front, and tie a bow or knot.

1 Attach the piece of burlap to the decorative piece of card stock with double-sided tape.

2 Secure the ribbon to the back of the decorative card stock, keeping the ribbon centered but approximately 1 inch (2.5 cm) from the bottom edge.

3 On the front of the decorative card stock, tie a granny knot and trim the ends of the ribbon.

4 Adhere to the folded note card and glue the swallow charm to the top of the knot.

GIFT DOUBLES AS DECORATION

Both a gift and a finishing decoration for this card, this ribbon slide charm is a nice present for that special someone. Make it yourself or secure any bracelet or necklace to the card with a little ribbon and a bow.

YOU WILL NEED

- 1 olive green ⅜-inch (1 cm)-wide grosgrain ribbon, 9 inches (23 cm)

- 1 magenta 1-inch (2.5 cm)-wide grosgrain ribbon, 9 inches (23 cm)

- double-sided tape

- 1 ribbon slide charm

- 1 toggle bracelet closure (optional, for handmade bracelet)

- 1 sheet decorative paper, 3½ x 5 ½ inches (9 x 14 cm)

- 1 sheet olive green card stock, 4 x 6 inches (10 x 15 cm)

- 1 white folded note card, 5 x 7 inches (12.5 x 17.8 cm)

- 1 pink chiffon ribbon, 7 inches (17.8 cm)

- 1 pair jewelry pliers (optional, for handmade bracelet)

- scissors

1 Layer the olive green ribbon over the magenta ribbon and adhere with double-sided tape.

2 Thread the ribbon slide charm onto the ribbon and add the toggle closure using jewelry pliers.

3 Adhere the decorative paper to the olive card stock and adhere to the folded card. Use the chiffon ribbon to secure the bracelet around the card by tying into a bow. Trim the ends.

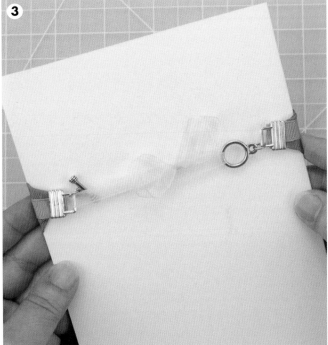

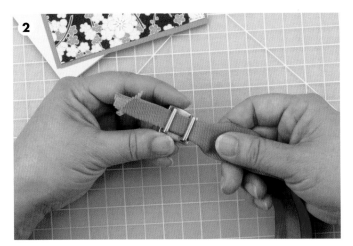

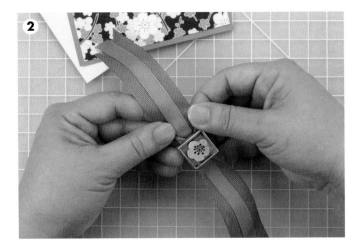

YOU WILL NEED

- 2 mizuhiki paper cords in red and gold, 50 cm (19.7 inch) (they typically come in metric measurements)

- masking tape

- 1 strip card stock to match folded notecard, 1¼ x 4 inches (3.1 x 10 cm)

- adhesive

- 1 sheet decorative paper, 5¼ x 4 inches (13.4 x 10 cm)

- 1 white folded note card, 5½ x 4¼ inches (14 x 10.8 cm)

Mizuhiki

When I first started using mizuhiki, or decorative paper cords, I only thought these pretty paper cords added a feeling of elegance, and were different (because they looked like colored wire) and made nice embellishments to my cards. After falling in love using them, my curiosity took over and I learned that they are traditionally used in Japan for cards or envelopes holding monetary and very special gifts. Apparently, many centuries ago, red and white cords were tied and knotted around a gift, indicating its safe and nontampered delivery. This tradition continued with the development of mizuhiki. This cord is made with washi paper that is dyed for color and stiffened with starch. Today, these cords are still used in the traditional Japanese art form of tying symbolic decorative knots. There are three basic knots:

1 *Musubikiri* are tied tightly and not meant to be untied. They are used for one-time events (like weddings, funerals, and for illness).

2 *Hanamusubi* are knots that can be tied and untied. This knot is used for recurring celebrations, like birthdays, anniversaries, and promotions.

3 *Awabi musubi* knots are loops loosely intertwined and woven, and if you pull on the ends, the knot will become tighter. Often used for friendship (growing closer), good health (getting stronger), and even good business relationships.

I also learned circles or loops are important. Loops are good luck symbols, because they are round, smooth, and come "full circle." Wedding gifts and cards typically have two or more loops. Conversely, sympathy cards often have their loops cut.

Mizuhiki cords are available in many different colors and finishes, including brightly colored Mylar, thin strands of silk, or painted. In Japan (and many parts of Asia), colors are important. Red and white indicate gifts; black and white (or white alone) is for sympathy; and yellow or gold indicates courage, aristocracy, and cheerfulness, to name just a few.

SHOELACE-STYLE BOW

Almost everyone can tie a shoe. This easy bow creates a nice card for anyone, especially for events that happen over and over again, like birthdays, baby showers, and congratulations for good grades.

1 Find the center of both paper cords by loosely bending in half.

2 Center and secure the paper cords with masking tape to the back of the card stock strip.

3 Wrap the ends of the cords to the front of the card stock strip.

4 Tie a single knot.

5 Loop around and tie a bow.

6 Adhere to the decorative paper and adhere to the folded card.

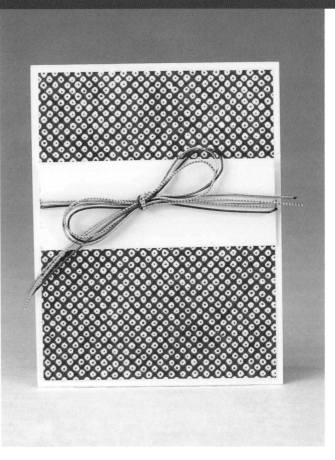

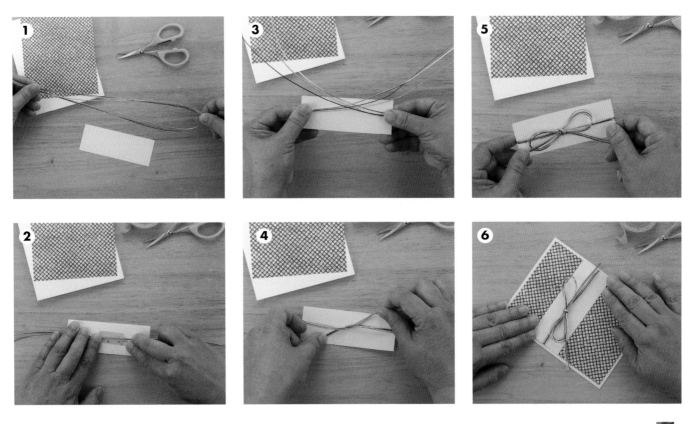

SIMPLE SQUARE KNOT

This is a fast yet elegant knot when used on a card. If following tradition, these are great for one-time events like weddings.

YOU WILL NEED

- adhesive

- 1 sheet decorative paper, 5 x 5 inches (12.5 x 12.5 cm)

- 1 white folded note card, 5½ x 5½ inches (14 x 14 cm)

- 3 strands mizuhiki paper cord in various colors to match decorative paper, 50 cm

- scissors

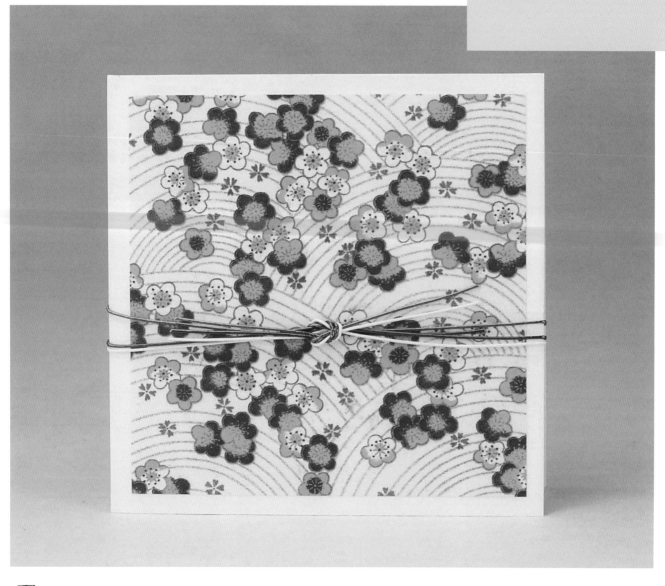

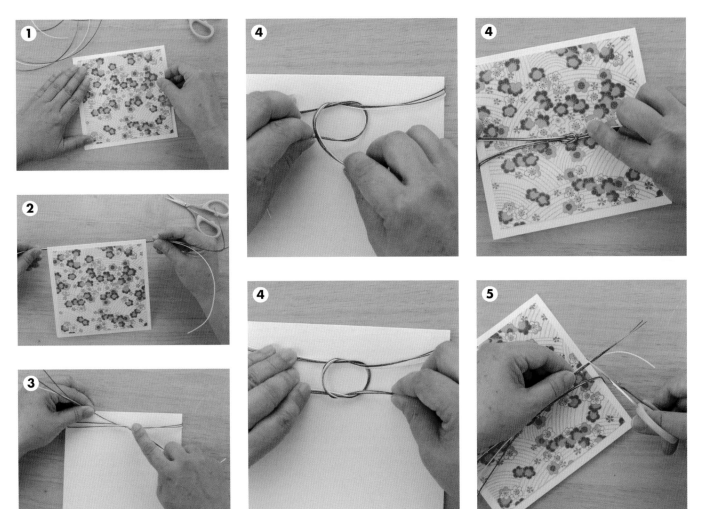

1 Adhere the decorative paper to the folded note card, leaving a ¼-inch (6 mm) margin on all sides.

2 Take all three strands of paper cord and gently bend in half to mark the center. Hang the folded card over the paper cords. Roughly align the center of the card with the middle of the strands. Bend the right side of the paper cords at the right edge of the card. Repeat on the left side.

3 Tie a square knot with the three cords. Wrap the right side of the cord over the left side, tuck it under, and pull them snug.

4 Take the left side and place it over the right side, tuck it under, and pull snug.

5 Clean up the ends of the cords by trimming with scissors. They look best if one is slightly shorter than the other.

Girl Scout Rhyme for a Square (Reef) Knot

I learned this when I was a Brownie: "Right over left, left over right, makes your knot both tidy and tight."

YOU WILL NEED

- 3 strands mizuhiki cords, 1 m (1 yard)

- adhesive

- 1 sheet decorative paper to match one of the colored cords, 2¼ x 2¼ inches (5.7 x 5.7 cm)

- 1 sheet cream card stock, 2¼ x 2¼ inches (5.7 x 5.7 cm)

- 1 pink folded note card, 3¾ x 8⅝ inches (9.5 x 22 cm)

- scissors

ABALONE KNOT

Abalone is a seafood delicacy associated with luxury. This complicated-looking knot resembles an abalone shell and makes a beautiful embellishment.

There are many suggestions on tying knots that use multiple strands of mizuhiki. One suggestion is to tie the knot loosely with one cord and add additional cords by following the pattern. For me, it is easier to tie everything at once. However, it would also be easier if you were an octopus with eight arms. To make the photos more understandable, I used a fabric cord that is flexible and keeps its shape. This helped the ends of the cord stay in place while taking the photos.

1 Start by holding the right side of the cord pointing upward. Take the left side of the cord and loop it over the upward-pointing end.

2 Make a second loop toward the left underneath the first loop and position the cord over the section pointing up.

3 Working from left to right, thread the cord under the rightmost cord, over the next, under the third, and finally over the last cord.

4 Gently pull the loops tighter by moving the ends of the cords outward.

5 Trim the ends so they graduate in length.

6 Adhere the decorative paper to the cream-colored paper at a 45-degree angle, making this look like a diamond shape, and adhere both pieces to the note card approximately 1 inch (2.5 cm) from the upper edge. Adhere the abalone knot in the center of the square layers. It is traditional to keep the ends turned upward. This implies that the knot keeps all the happiness given with the card.

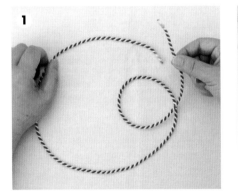

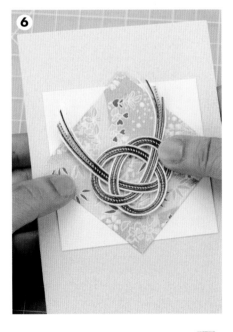

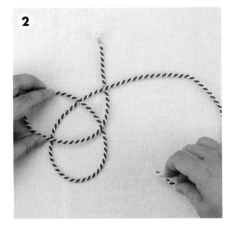

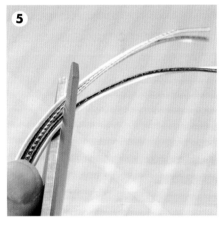

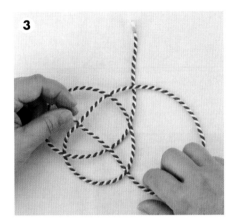

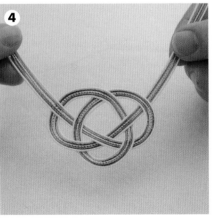

KNOTTED HEARTS

A couple of loops tied together creates a heart, a unique embellishment
to add to the card for someone you love.

YOU WILL NEED

- 3 strands mizuhiki cords in red, blue, and sparkling black

- double-sided tape

- 1 sheet decorative card stock, 4½ x 4½ inches (11.4 x 11.4 cm)

- 1 navy blue folded note card, 5½ x 5½ inches (14 x 14 cm)

- adhesive

- scissors

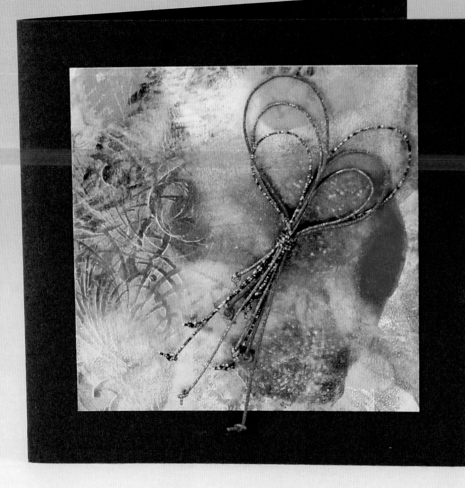

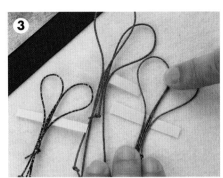

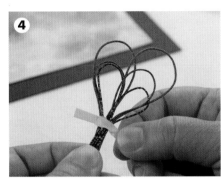

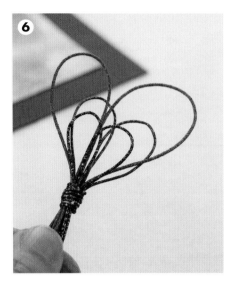

1 Cut the red mizuhiki paper cord into two 10-inch (25.4 cm) segments. Cut the blue cord into two 8-inch (20 cm) segments and cut the sparkling black cord into two 6-inch (15.2 cm) segments. Tie each end in a single knot.

2 Gather the two ends of one cord and create a loop. Repeat with the second cord in the same color and adhere with a thin piece of double-sided tape, forming a heart shape. It looks best if the ends of the cord are not the same length.

3 Repeat for the next two colors of cord.

4 Layer the three hearts in graduating sizes, with the largest heart at the bottom. Wrap the base of the three hearts together with a thin strip of double-sided adhesive tape.

5 Cover the tape by wrapping with the sparkling black cord five or six times.

6 Tuck in the ends and trim with scissors.

7 Adhere the decorative card stock to the folded notecard and glue the knotted hearts to the card.

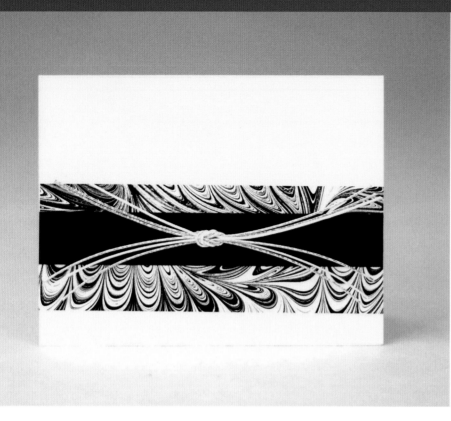

YOU WILL NEED

- 3 strands mizuhiki paper cord, 50 cm (19.7 inch)

- adhesive

- 1 strip black card stock, ¾ x 5½ inches (2 x 14 cm)

- 1 sheet black-and-white marble-patterned paper, 2½ x 5½ inches (6.4 x 14 cm)

- 1 white folded note card, 5½ x 4¼ inches (14 x 10.8 cm)

- scissors

SYMPATHY KNOT

Loops can symbolize the "circle of life" — sustainable, infinite. They are good things, but the opposite can be implied if the loop is cut. An event that happens once, preferably not repeated. When paired with black and white, it is a heartfelt way to send your sympathies.

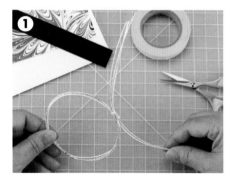

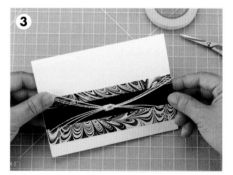

1 Using all three strands of mizuhiki, tie a square knot, leaving 3-inch (7.5 cm) tails. This creates a loop.

2 Cut the loop in half at the point opposite the knot. Trim the ends to approximately 3 inches (7.5 cm). It looks best if all the ends are the same length.

3 Adhere the black strip to the patterned paper and adhere to the folded card. Adhere the knot to the black paper.

YOU WILL NEED

- black ink pad
- 1 magazine page in a contrasting color
- adhesive
- 1 sheet decorative card stock, 3 x 4½ inches (7.5 x 11.4 cm)
- 1 strand mizuhiki paper cord in gold
- 1 sheet red card stock, 4 x 6 inches (10 x 15.2 cm)
- 1 white folded note card, 5 x 7 inches (12.5 x 17.8 cm)
- rubber stamp of butterfly
- scissors
- pencil

BUTTERFLY ANTENNAE

I have a hard time cutting out butterfly shapes with their antennae. The mizuhiki paper cord makes the perfect curl for the antennae, and it's really bright, shiny, and pretty.

1 Stamp 3 butterflies onto the magazine page and cut out with scissors. It is okay to cut off the antennae. Adhere to the decorative card stock.

2 Cut 6 inches (15.2 cm) of paper cord. Curl the ends around a pencil for the right diameter of curl.

3 Pinch in half and twist so the curled ends face outward.

4 Adhere to the butterflies on the decorative card stock, adhere to the red card stock, and then adhere to the folded card.

YOU WILL NEED

- 3 different colors or patterns of washi or decorative tape, each 12 inches (30.5 cm)
- 1 sheet white card stock, 4¼ x 6¼ inches (10.8 x 16 cm)
- 1 strand mizuhiki paper cord, 12 inches (30.5 cm)
- adhesive
- 1 sheet black card stock, 4½ x 6½ inches (11.4 x 16.5 cm)
- 1 white folded note card, 5 x 7 inches (12.5 x 17.8 cm)
- bamboo skewer
- scissors

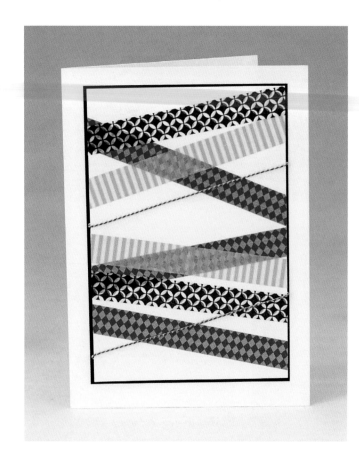

Masking Tape: Decorative, Fun, and Whimsical

It is amazing how a frustrated auto mechanic and a creative chemist changed how we decorate cards. Well, not directly. In the mid-1920s, a lab assistant (Richard G. Drew) at Scotch 3M was inspired by complaints from an auto body shop. The butcher paper used to block paint from certain parts of the car when it was painted was not working properly. The unwanted paint had to be removed by hand, which was tedious and time consuming. A pressure-sensitive, gentler adhesive tape was invented. More recently, a couple of clever Japanese crafters showed their masking tape company the fun and decorative uses for the tape, and today we have hundreds of printed decorative tapes to use for making fun and interesting cards.

DIAGONAL WRAPPING

Angles add interest, and with some metallic-colored paper cord, this card is perfect for anyone.

1. Pull off approximately 5 inches (12.5 cm) of decorative tape (red) and apply to the white card stock at an angle.

2. Wrap around to the back of the paper and secure.

3. Continue with the first color (red) two more times, applying the tape in a zigzag pattern. Repeat with the other two colors of tape, positioning the tape at diagonals, making sure to overlap.

4. Apply a thin line of glue to the card using a bamboo skewer.

5. Adhere the paper cord and trim to the edge of the card. Repeat approximately 3 inches (7.5 cm) below.

6. Adhere to the black card stock and adhere to the white folded card.

YOU WILL NEED

- 1 sheet white card stock, 3¾ x 5 inches (9.5 x 12.5 cm)

- 4–5 colors and patterns decorative tape

- twine, 12 inches (30.5 cm)

- adhesive

- 1 sheet orange card stock, 4 x 5¼ inches (10 x 13.3 cm)

- 1 white folded note card, 4¼ x 5½ inches (10.8 x 14 cm)

- wax paper

- scissors

PENNANT FLAG BANNER

Pennant flags are symbolic of fun and whimsy. Use colorful and decorative printed tape to easily create the pennant flags.

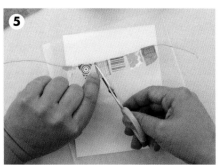

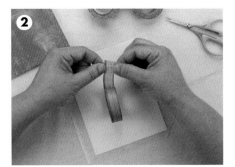

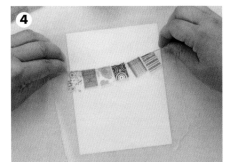

Nothing Goes to Waste

When I was trimming the corners of the tape to make the pennant flags, I had a lot of cute little pieces left over. It was easier to just stick these bits to a piece of paper while I was working, instead of putting them into the trash. The result was a decorative background sheet for a different card.

1 Set the wax paper on top of the white card stock. At this point, the white card stock is a guide for how long to make the pennant banner.

2 Place the first piece of tape approximately 3 inches (7.5 cm) from the end of the twine. Overlap ⅜ inch (1 cm) of the tape onto the twine so that the tape wraps the twine and sticks to itself.

3 Trim the tape about 1 inch (2.5 cm) long. Stick it to the wax paper.

4 Repeat, making sure to alternate colors and patterns of tape, until the flags stop at the right edge of the card.

5 Trim the tape diagonally from the middle of the tape to each edge nearest to the attached twine, making a triangle.

6 Duplicate the banner so there are two pennant banners. Adhere the points of pennants of the first banner to the white card stock. Tuck in the ends of the twine and adhere to the back.

7 Repeat for the second banner so it drapes across the first banner at an angle. Adhere this piece to the orange-colored card stock and adhere to the folded card.

ADORN A PHOTO

Sending a photo on a card is fun, meaningful, and easy when using decorative tape to attach the photo.

YOU WILL NEED

- 1 sheet black-and-white gingham card stock, 4 x 5 inches (10 x 12.5 cm)
- 1 white folded note card, 5 x 7 inches (12.5 x 17.8 cm)
- double-sided tape
- 1 photo
- 2 strips pink floral decorative tape, 2 inches (5 cm)

1 Secure the printed card stock to the folded card with double-sided tape.

2 Lay the photo on the printed card stock and secure the opposing corners with decorative tape.

3 Tear the tape pieces instead of cutting them to create a feeling of whimsy, which matches the mood of the photo.

ASYMMETRICALLY WOVEN

Slightly askew and off center seems to break the rules, but the results are interesting and bold in this cute, contemporary design.

YOU WILL NEED

- 5 strips decorative tape in 3 different patterns, each 5 inches (12.5 cm)
- 1 sheet white card stock, 3¾ x 5 inches (9.5 x 12.5 cm)
- embroidery floss in a color that contrasts the buttons
- 3 buttons in colors that match the tape
- adhesive
- double-sided tape
- 1 blue folded note card, 4¼ x 5½ inches (10.8 x 14 cm)
- scissors

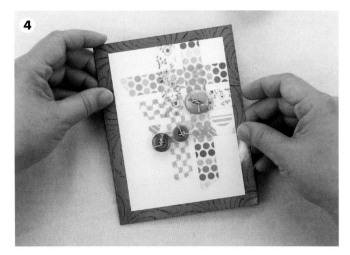

1 Horizontally lay three strips of different patterned tape onto the white card stock with the first strip starting 1 inch (2.5 cm) below the top of the card. Keep the left end ¼ inch (6 mm) from the left edge of the card and wrap the right end of the tape over the right edge, securing it to the back. Repeat with the next two strips, ⅛ inch (3 mm) below the first and to the left, graduating ⅛ to ¼ inch (3 to 6 mm).

2 Vertically lay two strips following the horizontal pattern, alternating different decorative strips.

3 Thread the embroidery floss though a button and tie a knot at the top of the button. Trim the thread and repeat with the other two buttons. Glue the buttons to the intersections of the decorative tape.

4 Adhere to the folded card with double-sided tape.

FREE-FORM STRIPED HEART

Making this heart-shaped image is self-explanatory, but I found a way of making this style card very efficient.

YOU WILL NEED

- 5 strips decorative tape in different patterns but within the same color family, each 3½ inches (9 cm)
- 1 white folded note card, 4¼ x 5½ inches (10.8 x 14 cm)
- 1 piece wax paper at least 4¼ x 5½ inches (10.8 x 14 cm)
- bone folder
- scissors
- rubber stamp of heart (optional)
- permanent black ink pad (optional)

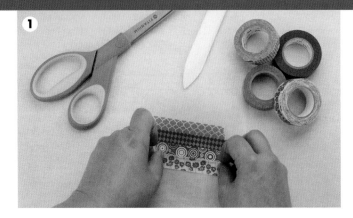

1 Lay one strip of decorative tape approximately 1 inch (2.5 cm) from the top of the wax paper. Continue with each of the different patterns of tape, making sure each strip slightly overlaps the strip before. Use a bone folder to add pressure to secure the tape where it overlaps the next layer.

2 Cut out the shape of a heart.

3 Carefully peel the layers of tape starting from the top down. The heart shape should come off as one piece—so efficient!

4 Apply the heart to the folded card.

Wax Paper Is Transparent

If you are unsure about cutting out a heart shape, you can trace a heart by laying the wax paper over a printed or rubber-stamped heart. You can also rubber stamp a heart directly onto the wax paper if you use a permanent (solvent-based) ink.

YOU WILL NEED

- 1 white folded note card, 4¼ x 5½ inches (10.8 x 14 cm)
- 4 colors decorative tape, with one color being yellow, each 3 inches (7.5 cm)
- scissors

DRAWING WITH TAPE

There are so many different colors and patterns of decorative tape. With a little imagination and an eye for an object in its simplest form—rectangle, ellipse, circle, square—it is possible to create images that represent special events or occasions using the tape as the drawing medium.

1 With scissors, square off one end of the tape. Apply the tape to the folded card approximately 1 inch (2.5 cm) from the edge.

2 Tear off at approximately 2½ inches (6.4 cm). Repeat for the second and third colors.

3 Cut three teardrop shapes from the yellow tape and adhere to the tops of the three vertical strips, creating the flames for three candles.

Variation: Tannenbaum

Christmas trees are a popular icon for the season, and with so many different styles, you are sure to make loved ones smile when they receive a Christmas tree made from decorative tape.

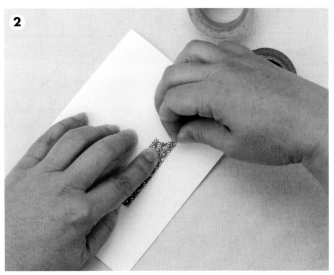

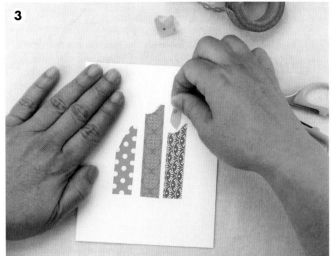

Cutout Shapes

Handheld punches and personal die-cutting machines have evolved into a vast array of shapes, designs, and sizes. Combine even the simplest of shapes with a little imagination to create these clever greetings.

SYMBOLIC DOMESTICATION

An apron is the practical article of clothing that protects garments worn underneath. Traditionally used by women, aprons are now equally popular with backyard barbecue moguls. Together on a card, they represent domestic bliss, perfect for a wedding anniversary or an invitation for the unveiling of that new grill.

YOU WILL NEED

- 1 sheet yellow gingham cardstock, 4 x 2 inches (10 x 5 cm)

- 1 doily

- adhesive

- ⅛-inch (3 mm)-wide yellow satin ribbon, 4 inches (10 cm)

- 1 sheet blue-striped card stock, 4 x 3 inches (10 x 7.5 cm)

- foam adhesive squares

- ⅛-inch (3 mm)-wide blue satin ribbon, 3 inches (7.5 cm)

- 1 sheet polka-dot card stock, 4 x 5¼ inches (10 x 13.3 cm)

- 1 white folded note card, 4¼ x 5½ inches (10.8 x 14 cm)

- ruler

- pencil

- handheld punches, ¾-inch (2 cm) square and 2½-inch (6.4 cm) circle

- scissors

- penknife

- cutting mat

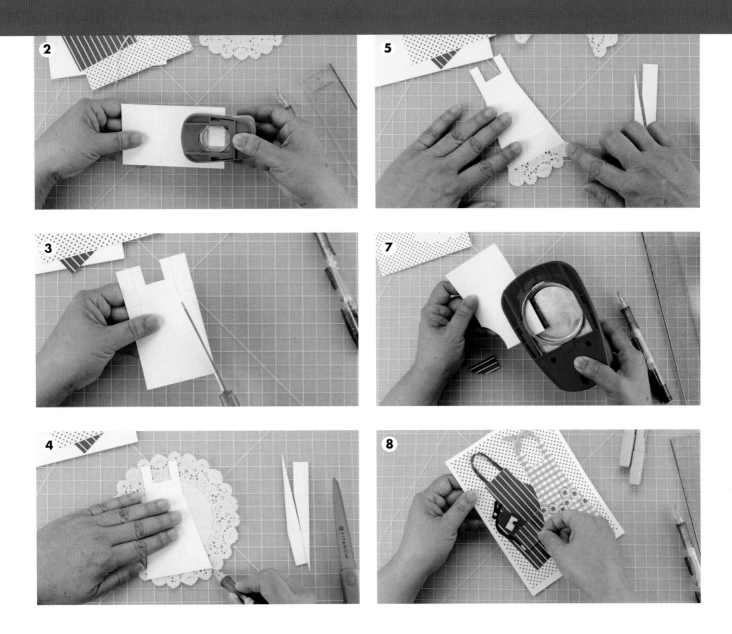

1 Create the feminine apron using the yellow gingham card stock. With the card stock positioned vertically in front of you, mark the center point with a ruler and draw a vertical guideline on the back in pencil.

2 Using the ¾-inch (2 cm) square punch, cut a square that is centered and along the top edge.

3 Draw a vertical guideline ¼ inch (6 mm) to the right and left of the square cutout and 1½ inches (3.8 cm) long. Draw two diagonal guidelines to the bottom corners of the card and cut out with scissors.

4 Position the bottom edge of the apron along the scalloped edge of the doily.

5 Trim to fit and adhere the doily, creating a lace ruffle at the bottom of the apron.

6 Tie together the ends of the yellow ribbon and secure the loop along the neckline and on the back of the apron.

7 Create the masculine apron using the blue-striped card stock. Punch the top corners with the circle punch, creating two quarter-circle cutouts.

8 With a penknife and cutting mat, cut two rectangular pieces from the punched quarter circles and apply to the apron with foam squares. Use the blue ribbon to make the ties. Adhere both aprons to the polka-dot card stock and then adhere to the card.

YOU WILL NEED

- 3 sheets decorative card stock, 2 x 2½ inches (5 x 6.4 cm)
- 1 sheet wood veneer decorative paper
- double-sided tape
- 1 strand mizuhiki paper cord
- adhesive
- 1 white folded note card, 5 x 7 inches (12.5 x 17.8 cm)
- ruler
- pencil
- handheld punches, ¾-inch (2 cm) and 1½-inch (3.8 cm) circles
- scissors

ONESIE CLOTHESLINE

Everything about a baby is cute, and this fun onesie shape is created with a couple of circles and a pair of scissors.

Hide the Glue

Because the mizuhiki paper cord is very thin, it is hard to hide the glue used to attach the cord to the card. You can strategically place the drops of glue and hide them behind the mini clothespins.

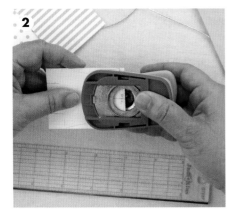

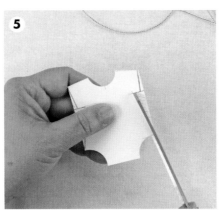

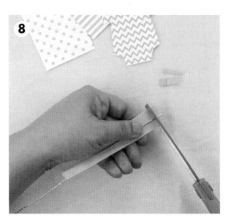

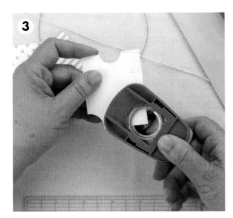

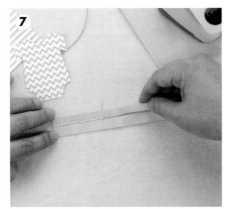

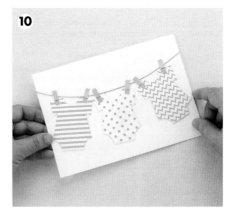

1 Cut a 2 x 2½-inch (5 x 6.4 cm) rectangle of card stock.

2 For the neckline, punch a half circle at the center top using the ¾-inch (2 cm) circle punch.

3 For the leg openings, punch a quarter circle at the bottom corners.

4 To slope the shoulders, make an angled cut from ¼ inch (6 mm) down on each side to the neckline.

5 Make ½ inch (1.3 cm) cut inward, 1 inch (2.5 cm) from the top on each side, forming the sleeves. Then cut ¼ inch (6 mm) from the side of each leg opening to the underarm to shape the sides.

6 Repeat steps 1 through 5 to make two more onesies from the remaining sheets of decorative card stock, and set aside.

7 To make the clothespins, cut two strips of wood veneer paper, one measuring ¼ x 3 inches (6 mm x 7.5 cm) and the other ⅜ x 3 inches (1 x 7.5 cm). Cut a 3-inch (7.5-cm) length of double-sided tape, place sticky side up and in the landscape position. adhere the narrower strip along the top edge of the tape. Follow this with the mizuhiki paper cord and then the wider strip.

8 Cut into ¼-inch (6 mm) pieces to create mini clothespins. Peel the backing off the double sided tape on the clothespins, and adhere to the shoulders of the onesies.

9 Place a small drop of glue on the left and right edges of the note card approximately 1 inch (2.5 cm) from the top. Adhere the mizuhiki cord at the left and right edges, drooping slightly.

10 Apply double-sided tape to the back of each onesie and adhere to the mizuhiki clothesline.

FOUR SEASONS

There is something comforting about the changing of the seasons. This card represents the predictability with a tree filled with snowflakes, leaves, flowers, and falling leaves.

YOU WILL NEED

- 1 each small sheet colored paper in green, light green, pink, white, yellow, orange, and brown

- adhesive

- 1 magazine or antique book page, 4½ x 7½ inches (11.4 x 19 cm), quartered

- 1 kraft-colored folded note card, 5½ x 8½ inches (14 x 21.6 cm)

- 1 white folded card, 5½ x 8½ inches (14 x 21.6 cm)

- handheld punches in leaf, snowflake, and flower shapes

- rubber stamp of tree frame, or print of 4 bare trees

- scissors

- black ink pad (optional, if using rubber stamp)

1 Punch the shapes from colored paper: leaves from green, light green, yellow, orange, and brown paper; flowers from pink paper; and snowflakes from white paper.

2 Stamp four trees onto the brown paper and cut out or cut out the four tree shapes from the print. Set aside.

3 Adhere the quartered pieces of magazine or book page to the folded card. Leave an ⅛-inch (3 mm) gap between the pieces with a larger margin around the edges.

4 Adhere the bare tree to the four panels and then each punched element: snowflakes on one panel; light green leaves and flowers on a second panel; green and light green leaves on a third panel; and yellow, orange, and brown leaves on a fourth panel. Add several brown leaves at the base of the fourth panel to represent fallen leaves.

Stay Organized with Little Trays

Keeping the different punched shapes separate makes this card fun and easy. Like painting a house, most of the work is in the preparation.

CIRCLE TAGS AND PEEK-A-BOO SPOTS

These floating circles make this card whimsical and fun. Layer them over a contrasting color for added emphasis. Gather up all your hole punches and punch away.

YOU WILL NEED

- 1 print of the words "hello," "hallo," and "bonjour" or in the language of your choice
- 1 sheet brown card stock, large enough to punch 3 circles
- adhesive
- silver cording, 24 inches (61 cm)
- 1 sheet striped card stock, 3½ x 8¼ inches (9 x 21.7 cm)
- 1 sheet white card stock, 3½ x 8¼ inches (9 x 21.7 cm)
- ⅜-inch (1 cm)-wide ribbon, 15 inches (38 cm)
- 1 white folded note card, 3¾ x 8⅝ inches (9.5 x 22 cm)
- handheld hole punches, ⅛, ¼, ⅜ (long reach), ¾, 1, and 1¼ inches (3 mm, 6 mm, 1 cm, 2 cm, 2.5 cm, and 3.2 cm)
- scissors

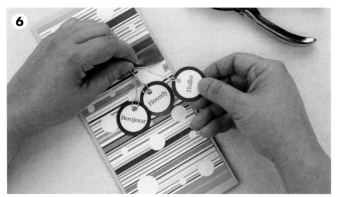

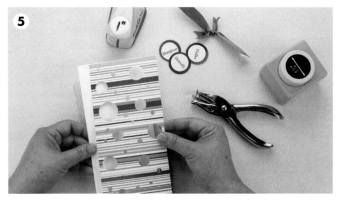

1 Make the round tags by first punching the printed words with the 1-inch (2.5 cm) punch.

2 Make the frame for the tags by punching the brown card stock with the 1¼-inch (3.2 cm) punch.

3 Adhere the cutout words to the brown circles to create framed circle tags. Punch with the ⅛-inch (3 mm) punch and thread onto a 3-inch (7.5 cm) loop of silver cording. Tie a knot in the cording. Repeat for all three round tags and set aside.

4 Using the striped sheet of card stock, randomly punch holes. Start with the large holes first and fill in with the smaller holes.

5 Adhere the striped card stock to the white card stock.

6 Wrap the ribbon around the back of the two layers and tie a knot on the front of the card, making sure to capture the stringed word tags. Adhere this layer to the folded card.

LADYBUG WITH SECRET MESSAGE

This little ladybug cleverly holds a secret message.

YOU WILL NEED

- 1 white mailing label, 4 x 2 inches (10 x 5 cm)

- 1 sheet green decorative card stock, 4 x 5¼ inches (10 x 13.3 cm)

- 1 sheet black card stock, 4 x 3 inches (10 x 7.5 cm)

- 1 sheet red card stock, 4 x 4 inches (10 x 10 cm)

- 1 strand mizuhiki paper cord or flexible wire, 5 inches (12.5 cm)

- double-sided tape

- 2 brads, ⅛ inch (3 mm)

- 1 white folded note card, 4¼ x 5½ inches (10.8 x 14 cm)

- circle punches, 2⅝ and 2 inches (6.7 and 5 cm)

- ruler

- penknife

- cutting mat

- corner rounder punch

- pencil

- flower punch, ⅜ inch (1 cm)

1. Using the 2⅝-inch (6.7 cm) circle punch, cut out a circle from the mailing label and adhere to the green card stock.

2. Punch a 2-inch (5 cm) circle from the black card stock and trim approximately ½ inch (1.3 cm) off. Punch a 2⅝-inch (6.7 cm) circle from the red card stock and cut in half using a ruler with a penknife on a cutting mat.

3. Make the antennae for the ladybug by pinching the mizuhiki or wire in half and curling the ends around a pencil. Attach to the back of the black partial circle with double-sided tape.

4. Adhere to the top of the white circle on the printed card stock.

5. Using the corner punch, trim one corner of each red half circle. To punch both at the same time, place the paper right sides together. This will ensure the cuts are mirrored.

6. Assemble the wings of the ladybug and secure with the brads.

7. Decorate the ladybug with flower shapes punched in black paper. Adhere the green card stock to the note card.

8. Spread the wings to reveal the perfect location to write a secret message.

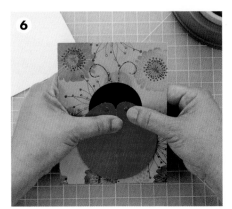

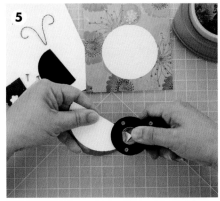

YOU WILL NEED

- 3 magazine pages in greens and blues, enough to cover 4 x 5¼ inches (10 x 13.3 cm)

- 1 sheet white card stock, 4 x 5¼ inches (10 x 13.3 cm)

- paper adhesive

- 20 white paper strips, ⅛ x 11 inches (3 mm x 28 cm)

- 4 black paper strips, ⅛ x 11 inches (3 mm x 28 cm)

- 1 white folded note card, 4¼ x 5½ inches (10.8 x 14 cm)

- quilling tool

- bamboo skewer

- broad sponge brush

- scissors

Quilling or Paper Filigree

This craft involves strips of paper that are rolled and shaped, creating beautiful designs. It was developed by Renaissance nuns and monks, who took strips of vellum trimmed during the gilding process and rolled them into filigree patterns. Today, quilling paper is available in precut strips in a rainbow of colors. Quilling art can be quite elaborate. These are more in the style of fun.

Common quilling shapes.

JUMPING SHEEP

One of the challenges of quilling is to think in circles. Sheep tend to be circular in shape, making them the perfect models.

1 Make the background by collaging magazine pages to the card stock sheet with the paper adhesive. To create a pasture scene, apply the blue colors toward the top and green toward the bottom.

2 Make the quill pieces from the white and black strips of paper using the quilling tool and dabs of glue applied with a bamboo skewer.

3 To make the little sheep, you will need approximately nine ⅜-inch (1 cm)-diameter white circles, eight ⅛-inch (3 mm)-diameter white circles, and six ⅜-inch (1 cm)-diameter loose black circles that will be flattened to make the ears and legs.

4 The dancing sheep needs nine ⅜-inch (1 cm)-diameter white circles; three ¼-inch (6 mm)-diameter white circles; six or seven ⅛-inch (3 mm)-diameter white circles; six ½-inch (1.3 cm)-diameter loose black to make the ears, legs, and arms; and five ⅛-inch (3 mm)-diameter black circles for the nose and hooves.

Coils Are Fun

Make these coils using a quilling tool and a ⅛-inch (3 mm) wide strip of paper. If it is a little sturdy it holds its shape, but thicker papers are also more difficult to roll. Using a quilling tool makes coils fast and without feeling like you have eight thumbs.

1 Insert strip into quilling tool's split tip.

2 Twirl the handle of the tool, coiling the paper.

3 Adhere the end of the paper coil with a little glue.

MONOGRAM

I like letters, both the kind I receive in the mail and those that I use to put together words. Stylish monograms are always fun to receive, and these initials are easily quilled.

YOU WILL NEED

- 12 paper strips, ⅛ x 12 inches (3 mm x 30.5 cm)
- adhesive
- 1 sheet black card stock, 3 x 3¼ inches (7.5 x 8.3 cm)
- 1 white folded note card, 3¾ x 8⅝ inches (9.5 x 22 cm)
- monogram print
- foam mat or board
- dressmaker's straight pins
- scissors
- bamboo skewer
- quilling tool
- tweezers (optional)

Inside the Curve

Always bending the paper strip around the curves works if the curve is convex. A concave or inside curve can be tricky. In these instances, the paper will hold better if it is wrapped around the opposite side of the pin.

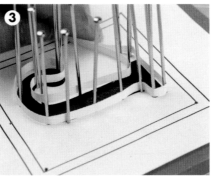

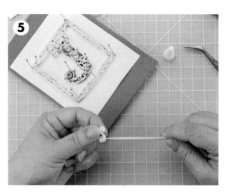

1 Secure the monogram print to the foam. Insert straight pins in the outer corners of the frame.

2 Bend one strip of paper around the outer guideline of the frame. While the paper strip is loose, pinch the corners where the paper wraps around the pin. Trim the paper to overlap about ½ inch (1.3 cm). Add a dab of glue with the bamboo skewer. Repeat with the interior frame.

3 Add pins to the outline of the letter. Wrap the paper strip around the pins, pinching the corners to make the corners square. Overlap the intersection by about ½ inch (1.3 cm) and glue.

4 Fill up the outlines with a variety of coiled strips, using the quilling tool. Mix up the coils. Make S-curves, teardrops, or single circles. The space between the frame is ⅛ inch (3 mm), so try to keep the coils small. Place the coils inside the frame to make sure you have enough and they all fit, using tweezers, if needed.

5 Carefully remove one coil at a time and apply adhesive to the points that will touch the frame or outline of the initial. Be neat with the glue, or you will adhere your coils to the pattern.

6 Remove the pins and adhere the frame and monogram to the black card stock. Adhere this to the folded card.

YOU WILL NEED

- paper strips in blue, light blue, brown, green, and yellow, 1/8 x 11 inches (3 mm x 28 cm)

- adhesive

- 1 sheet khaki card stock, 4 x 6 inches (10 x 15.2 cm)

- 1 white folded note card, 5 x 7 inches (12.5 x 17.8 cm)

- bamboo skewer

CURLY BLUE BIRD

This little birdie seems eager to tweet! For efficient crafting, roll and shape all of the little quilling components first and then assemble the image on the card.

1 Make the bird starting with the body. Create a 2-inch (5 cm) teardrop using the blue paper strip. With the ends facing the same direction, glue them together using a bamboo skewer to dab the glue. Make the head of the bird with a blue circle approximately 1 inch (2.5 cm) in diameter. Fill in the open areas of the body and head with smaller blue coils.

2 Make the tail by loosely making an S-curl and folding it in half.

3 Make the crest feathers by folding the blue paper strip in a zigzag pattern. Start with ¾ inch (2 cm) and vary the sizes, making four feathers. Leave at least ½ inch (1.3 cm) at either end and glue these together. Add a small drop of glue inside one of the pinched zigzags to secure. Adhere the crest to the head of the bird and then attach the head to the body.

4 Create the branches of the tree and the legs of the bird by curling the brown strips around the bamboo skewer.

5 Make leaves with the green paper by creating ¾- and ¼-inch (2 cm and 6 mm) coils and pinch opposite ends to create eye shapes.

6 Adhere all pieces to the khaki-colored card stock and adhere to the folded card.

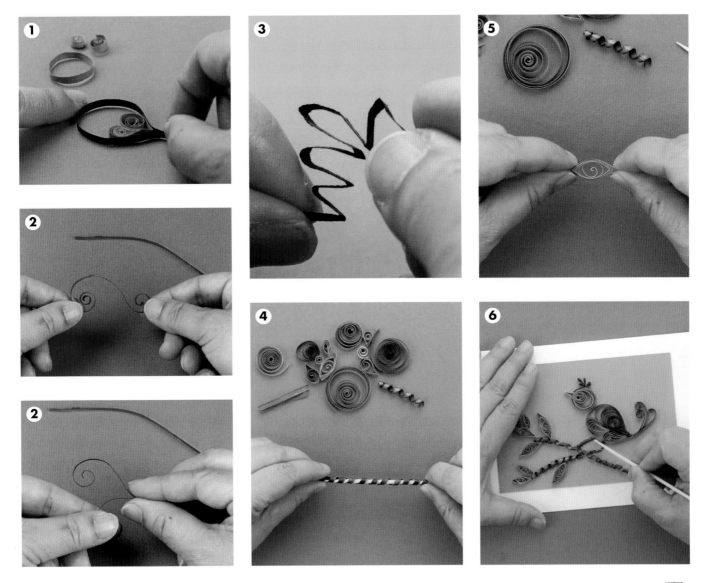

Folded Cards

Traditionally, a sheet of card stock folded in half makes a standard greeting card. However, it's always fun to be unique, and folding the card in different ways makes your handmade card special.

GATEFOLD KIMONO CARD

This style of card is similar to a pair of window shutters that opens from the middle and swings out. When opened, your message is framed just like looking in a window.

1. Orient the sheet of card stock horizontally in front of you and measure and score a vertical line at 2⅛ and 6⅜ inches (5.4 and 16.2 cm).

2. Fold the left panel to the right and fold the right panel to the left, with the edges meeting in the middle.

3. Decorate the paper with the panels closed. This keeps the pattern of the print aligned for both panels.

4. Create the band closure by laying the strip of colored card stock with approximately 1 inch (2.5 cm) hanging over the left edge of the right panel. Crease the band at the same point as the folded edge on the right side of the card. Wrap the left side of the band around the back of the card and around to the front, and crease the band at the fold on the left side of the card. The edges of this band should overlap at the center of the card. Place a small mark in the middle of the band at the center where the card closes.

5. Remove the band and, holding it so the right and left sides are overlapped, punch a small hole through these two layers at the center mark.

6. Open the band, and on the left side, cut the card stock from the edge to the punched hole. On the right side of the band, cut from the opposite edge to the punched hole.

7. Wrap the band around the card and close the band.

8. Stamp the kimono onto a scrap piece of card stock and cut out. Adhere the kimono to one side of the band, making sure to keep the vertical cut free of glue.

The Perfect Intersection

To make sure there will be no gap when panels are closed, fold the first panel. Then carefully align the second panel before creasing the fold. If the top and bottom of the panels are not square, carefully trim with a paper trimmer or penknife and ruler.

YOU WILL NEED

- 1 sheet decorative card stock, 8½ x 5½ inches (21.6 x 14 cm)

- 2 flowers cut from polka-dot paper, 3 inches (7.5 cm) wide

- double-sided tape

- 1 flower cut from contrasting pattern paper, 2½ inches (6.4 cm) wide

- 1 flower-shaped brad

- adhesive

- ruler

- scoring tool

- bone folder

- pencil

- hole punch (¹⁄₁₆ inch [1.5 mm] is best)

- scissors

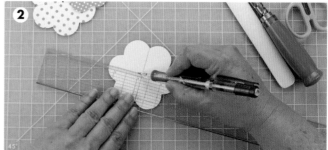

1 Orient the sheet of card stock horizontally in front of you and measure and score a vertical line at 2⅛ and 6⅜ inches (5.4 and 16.2 cm). Fold the left panel to the right and fold the right panel to the left, intersecting the edges in the center of the card. Set aside.

2 On one of the larger flowers, draw a guideline from the middle of the curve on one petal to the top of the curve on the opposite petal. Draw a perpendicular line connecting the indentations between the two petals. The intersection of these two lines is the center of the flower.

Little Hole (Somehow) Adds Strength

We might need to ask an engineer about this step, but a small hole at the end of a cut where tabs will be inserted into the cuts, helps keep the paper from tearing.

Stay in between the Lines

Try to keep the adhesive just inside the cut lines of the pieces being adhered. For this card, the flower will hang over the edge of the card and if the adhesive is exposed, it will adhere parts of the card to itself.

3 Punch a hole in the center of both larger flowers.

4 Cut through both of these flower shapes from the notch between the petals to the hole in the center of the flower. When the top flower is turned 180 degrees, these opposing cuts will slide together and create the closure for the card.

5 Lay the flower shapes face down in front of you with the slices in the flower pieces pointing in the same direction. Apply double-sided tape along one side of the slice on each flower.

6 Working with the printed sides of all pieces facing down, orient one flower where the slice in the flower is pointed toward the top of your work surface. Adhere the right side of the

folded card to the left side of the flower. Next, adhere the left edge of the card to the right side of the flower. The slice in this flower should be pointing down. Insert the slices together to close the card.

7 Add flower brad to smaller flower. With the adhesive only on the right side of the smaller flower, adhere to the right side of the larger flower attached to the left side of the card.

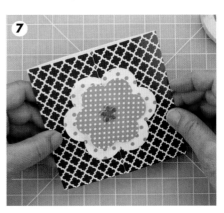

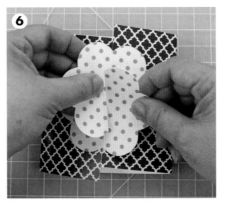

MOUNTAIN AND VALLEY FOLDS

This style of accordion fold identifies the upright folds as mountains and the lower folds as valleys. These cards are ideal for special occasions, because they can be displayed and admired.

YOU WILL NEED

- 1 sheet card stock printed on both sides, 12 x 12 inches (30.5 x 30.5 cm), cut in half

- adhesive

- cutout of a willow tree

- cutout of a Kokeshi doll

- 1 sheet decorative card stock, 4 x 5¼ inches (10 x 13.3 cm)

- 1½-inch (3.8 cm)-wide chiffon ribbon, 18 inches (45.7 cm)

- ruler

- scoring board

- bone folder

1. Position the first 6 x 12-inch (15.2 x 30.5 cm) card stock horizontally and measure and score at 4¼, 6⅜, 8½, and 11½ inches (10.8, 16.8, 21.6, and 29.2 cm). On the second sheet, score at 4¼, 8½, and 11½ inches (10.8, 16.8, and 21.6 cm). Fold along the scored lines in an accordion fashion by alternating the folds to make mountains and valleys.

2. Extend the card lengthwise by gluing the ½-inch (1.3 cm) flaps together. These accordion folds make mountains and valleys in graduating levels. Starting with the back panel, you should have a 4¼-inch (10.8 cm) mountain, a 3-inch (7.5 cm) mountain, and a 2⅛-inch (5.4 cm) mountain.

3. Adhere the willow tree to the front of the 3-inch (7.5 cm) mountain, making sure the top of the tree does not extend beyond the top of the card when folded. Add the doll to the front of the 2⅛-inch (5.4 cm) mountain with her head about ½ inch (1.3 cm) above the fold.

4. Add a patterned panel to the front of the card by adhering the decorative card stock to the back of the left side, leaving a ¼-inch (6 mm) margin.

5. Create a closure for the card by attaching a wide chiffon ribbon to the back of the card.

6. Wrap the ribbon from the back to the front of the card and tie a knot.

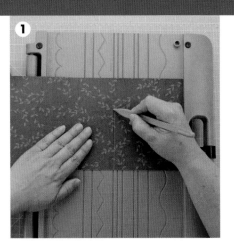

The Right Tool for the Job

Your time is important, and a scoring board is one of those tools that saves you time. Folding paper after using this tool is fast, and you will find making complicated folded cards easy.

TRI-FOLD SWEET SURPRISE

If you turn the mountain-and-valley folded card 90 degrees, the format changes, revealing a different look. The way this card is folded and assembled hides a secret message that is revealed when the card is opened.

YOU WILL NEED

- black ink pad
- 1 sheet lime green decorative card stock, 5¼ x 5¼ inches (13.4 x 13.3 cm)
- 1 sheet cream card stock, 5½ x 11 inches (14 x 28 cm)
- glue or double-sided tape
- cupcake image
- 1 sheet black damask decorative card stock, 5¼ x 2¾ inches (13.4 x 7 cm)
- 1 curly bracket frame cut from cream card stock, 3¾ x 2¾ inches (9.5 x 7 cm)

- 1 curly bracket frame cut from black card stock, 3¼ x 2¼ inches (8.3 x 5.7 cm)
- strip of black card stock, ¼ x 3 inches (6 mm x 7.5 cm), with corners rounded (creating an elongated ellipse)
- rubber stamp of swirls
- scoring board
- bone folder
- scissors
- white pen

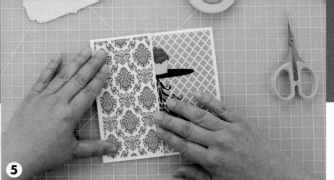

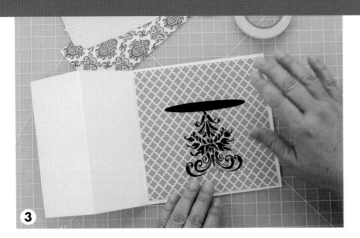

1 Stamp the swirled image onto the lime green card stock.

2 With the cream-colored sheet positioned horizontally in front of you, score vertically at 2¾ and 5½ inches (7 and 14 cm). Fold the 5½-inch (14 cm) scored line to the right. Fold the top panel at the 2¾-inch (7 cm) scored line to the left. Adhere the lime green paper to the 5½-inch (14 cm) square panel.

3 To create the table, adhere the elongated ellipse atop the swirled image.

4 Adhere the cupcake image on top of the table.

5 Adhere the black damask card stock to the folded front panel.

6 Adhere the black bracket frame to the center of the cream-colored bracket frame. Position the frame so it hides the cupcake and tabletop. Adhere the left side to the front panel. Be sure to keep the right side of the frame free of adhesive.

7 Add your message with the white pen.

Choose Strategic Areas

If using a brush marker to ink a rubber stamp, you can select a specific area of the design, which creates a different image when stamped.

YOU WILL NEED

- 2 sheets decorative card stock, 5½ x 17 inches (14 x 43.2 cm) and 4 x 5¼ inches (10 x 13.3 cm)

- 16 photo corners

- 4 photos, 2½ x 3½ inches (6.4 x 9 cm) in the portrait orientation

- adhesive

- die-cut cupcake with candle

- banner cut from vellum, 1 x 4¼ inches (2.5 x 10.8 cm)

- scoring board

- bone folder

ACCORDION-FOLDED PHOTO ALBUM

This is the perfect way to send those captured moments when the birthday girl had that first bite of birthday cake. This folded card will hold the snapshots of that moment.

1 Using the scoring board, score the large piece of card stock three times in 4¼-inch (10.8 cm) increments.

2 With the card lying face down horizontally in front of you, fold the card in half. Then fold the right panel to the left. Flip it over and fold the top panel to the left again. This is an accordion-folded card. Set aside.

3 Place a photo corner at each corner of each photo.

4 Adhere one photo to each of the four card panels.

5 Decorate the smaller card stock panel by adhering the die-cut cupcake and candle onto the card. Attach the banner.

6 With the accordion-folded card lying face down, adhere the cupcake panel to the right panel. This will be the front of the card.

FAUX V-NECK DRESS BODICE

Fold back the corner of the card to create a cute V-shaped neckline.

YOU WILL NEED

- 1 sheet decorative card stock, 5½ x 11 inches (14 x 28 cm)
- dye-based black ink pad
- 1 sheet white card stock, 4¼ x 5½ inches (10.8 x 14 cm)
- adhesive
- button
- scoring board
- ruler
- bone folder
- rubber stamp of lace or real lace trimming as long as it's flat
- scissors
- pencil

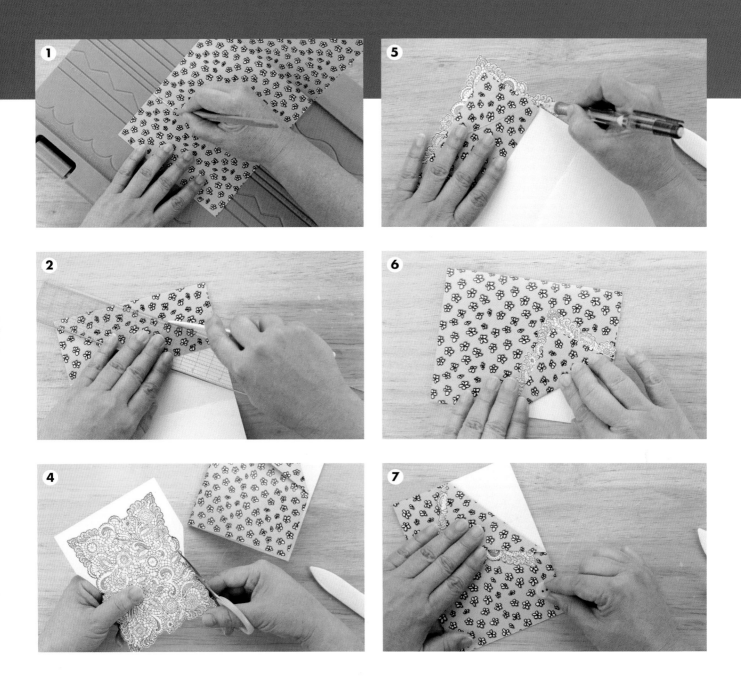

1 Orientate the decorative card stock horizontally and score at 2½ and 6¼ inches (6.4 and 16 cm). Starting from the left side, fold toward the right. When the card is folded, it will make a 4¼ x 5½-inch (10.8 x 14 cm) card.

2 Using the ruler and bone folder, score a line from the center of the top edge to the middle of the right folded edge.

3 Fold the upper-right corner toward the left. This will make the collar.

4 Rubber stamp the lace image with black ink onto the white card stock and cut out.

5 With the card open, lay the lace image under the tip of the collar. Align the corner of the lace image with the corner of the collar, allowing ½ inch (1.3 cm) of the lace edge to peek out behind the collar. Mark this piece where the card intersects with the stamped lace piece and cut from mark to mark.

6 Adhere to the back of the collar.

7 Glue on the button.

YOU WILL NEED

- 1 sheet card stock printed on both sides, 2½ x 2½ inches (6.4 x 6.4 cm)

- 1 brad, ⅛ inch (3 mm)

- adhesive

- 1 sheet decorative card stock, 3¾ x 5 inches (9.4 x 12.5 cm)

- 1 sheet brown card stock, 4 x 5¼ inches (10 x 13.3 cm)

- magenta folded note card, 4 ¼ x 5½ inches (10.8 x 14 cm)

- glue

- 1 bamboo skewer, 5 inches (12.5 cm)

- pencil

- ruler

- penknife

- cutting mat

- hole punch, ¹⁄₁₆ inch (1.5 mm)

PINWHEEL

These animated, colorful toys are reminders of breezy days with a lot of free time. Easy to re-create on a card, it sends the message of youth, fun, and happiness.

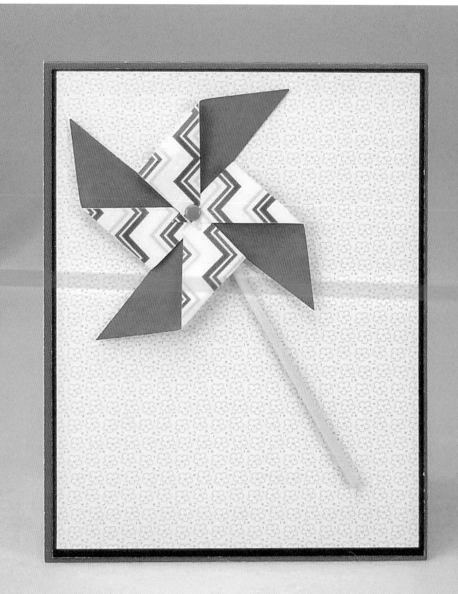

1. With a pencil and ruler, draw two diagonal lines on the 2½ x 2½-inch (6.4 x 6.4 cm) piece of card stock.

2. Cut 1¼ inches (3.1 cm) diagonally from the corner toward the center. Repeat on all for corners.

3. Punch a hole in the center of the square. Punch a hole in the left side of the split corner for each corner.

4. Starting with one corner, insert the brad into each corner hole. It is best to work in order.

5. Finish the pinwheel by inserting the brad into the center hole, and secure by separating and flattening the brad prongs.

6. Adhere the decorative card stock to the brown card stock and then adhere to the magenta card. Attach the pinwheel with glue on the bamboo skewer. It looks best to hide the point of the skewer under the pinwheel.

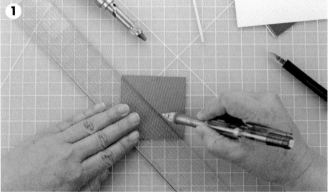

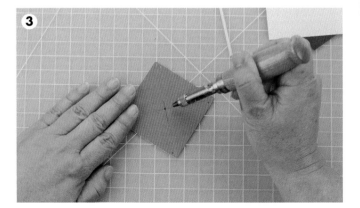

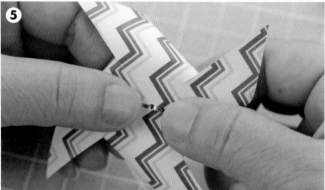

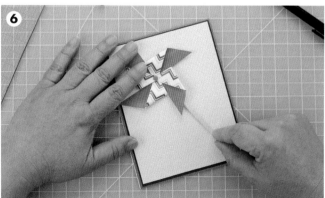

MASCULINE SHIRT

A cut here, a fold there, and this flat piece of card stock transforms into a fun card for the man in your life.

YOU WILL NEED

- 1 sheet light blue card stock, 4¼ x 8½ inches (10.8 x 21.6 cm)
- red dye-based ink pad
- 1 sheet white or cream card stock, 4¼ x 5½ inches (10.8 x 14 cm)
- adhesive foam tape
- ruler
- bone folder or scoring tool
- pencil
- scissors
- rubber stamp of bow tie or 2 bow-tie stickers
- hole punch, ¼ inch (6 mm)

Camouflage

When layering images, use the one you like the least for the bottom layer. It will be camouflaged, or hidden, by the nicer image.

Punch Upside Down

If you use the punch upside down, you can see the outline of the punch shape. This makes it easy to align the cutout to capture the printed design.

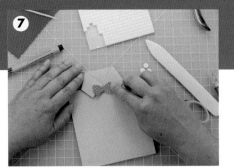

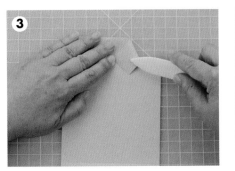

1 Position the light blue card stock horizontally in front of you. Starting from the left, measure and score the light blue card stock at the 5-inch (12.5 cm) point. Draw a guideline at 10 inches (25.4 cm), or 1 inch (2.5 cm) from the right edge.

2 Lay the card stock vertically in front of you with the 1-inch (2.5 cm) guideline toward you. Cut 1 inch (2.5 cm) from the edge of the card along the guideline. Mark the center point. Later, you will need a vertical guideline from this mark for the buttons.

3 Turn the paper so the 1-inch (2.5 cm) guideline is toward the top. Take the upper-left corner of the left tab and fold at an angle to intersect with the center guideline. Repeat with the upper-right corner.

4 Fold along the scored lines and tuck the edge under the collar corners. Set aside.

5 Stamp two bow ties with red ink onto the white card stock. Cut out both images and set one aside. Cut apart the second bow tie and discard the middle piece.

6 Adhere the right and left sides of the bow tie using the foam tape. This creates a 3D effect.

To make the bow tie look a little more realistic, attach it at the center mark along the intersection of the shirt collar.

7 Adhere the bow tie to the top panel between the collar corners.

8 Create three buttons for the shirt. First draw four little dots in a square pattern about 2 mm apart. Repeat two more times. Punch this square of dots using the hole punch.

9 Adhere the buttons to the center guideline, spacing them approximately 1 inch (2.5 cm) apart.

YOU WILL NEED

- 1 sheet white card stock
  8½ x 11 inches
  (21.6 x 28 cm)
- 1 sheet red card stock
  8½ x 11 inches
  (21.6 x 28 cm)
- Yin Yang Heart pattern
  (page 250)
- adhesive
- penknife
- cutting mat
- scoring tool
- ruler
- bone folder
- scissors

YIN YANG HEART

"How did they do that?" A simple heart shape where the cleavage

of the heart intersects makes this card appear complicated.

1 Trace the pattern on page 250 and transfer it to the back of each sheet of card stock.

2 With a penknife and cutting mat, cut out the smaller hearts from the center of the larger hearts.

3 Cut out the large heart shapes and the card edges. Score along the center score line.

4 Fold over the card panels.

5 Flip one card 180 degrees and intersect the two opposing heart shapes at the indentation point, or cleavage.

6 Flip over the card and lift one side. Glue the two panels together.

7 Close the card by intersecting the hearts.

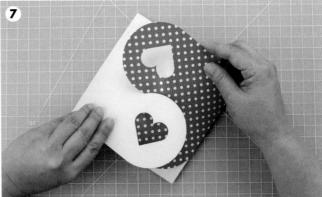

IRIS FOLDING

This style of card was developed in the Netherlands and is called "iris folding." The pattern for the finished card resembles the iris or the lens of a camera.

YOU WILL NEED

- 1 card stock frame, 3½ x 3½ inches (8.9 x 8.9 cm) with a ½-inch (1.3 cm) margin
- masking tape
- 8 strips of 4 different colors lightweight printed paper, 1 x 5 inches (2.5 x 12.5 cm), folded lengthwise
- double-sided tape or paste glue
- 1 sheet decorative card stock, 5¼ x 5¼ inches (13.4 x 13.4 cm)
- 1 folded note card, 5½ x 5½ inches (14 x 14 cm)
- 1 dark brown paper band, 5½ x 3 inches (14 x 7.5 cm)
- iris fold pattern (page 248)
- scissors

Focus on the Center

Often a little trinket, rhinestone, button, or other embellishment is glued in the center of the iris folded piece.

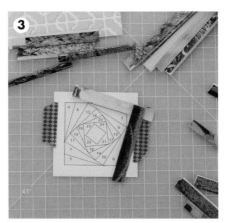

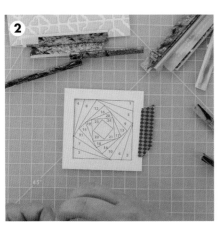

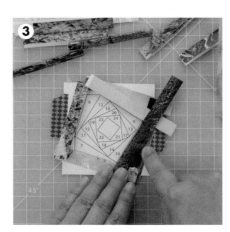

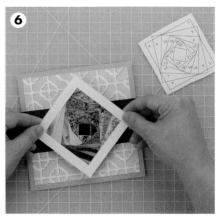

1 Lay the iris fold pattern on a nonstick surface, and place the card stock frame on top.

2 Secure to the table (nonstick surface) with masking tape.

3 Following the pattern, lay the first folded strip over section 1 and use double-sided tape to adhere to the frame. Lay down the second strip (in a different color) at section 2, again taping to the frame. Continue following the pattern, taping each new strip to the previous strips.

4 Carefully peel up the iris folded pattern piece and remove the masking tape.

5 Trim all the strips that extend past the frame.

6 Adhere the decorative sheet to the folded card and adhere the band. Adhere the iris folded piece to the card.

YOU WILL NEED

- 3 sheets origami paper in 3 colors and graduating sizes
- adhesive
- 1 sheet patterned washi paper, 4½ x 4½ inches (11.4 x 11.4 cm)
- 1 folded note card, 5½ x 5½ inches (14 x 14 cm)
- bone folder (optional)

Origami: The Art of Paper Folding

Origami began in Japan in the seventh century, when Buddhist monks brought paper to Japan from China. At the time, paper was very precious, so these folded objects were used for religious purposes and special occasions.

CRANES

The origami crane is a symbol of good health, but its meaning began to include "wishes for world peace" after a Hiroshima survivor (Sadako Sasaki, twelve years old) inspired others. She was diagnosed with leukaemia ten years after the bombing, and Sadako was told her wish for good health would come true if she folded 1,000 cranes. She almost made it, but not quite. Her school friends continued her mission and folded the remaining 366 to make the final count 1,000 to be buried with her. Sadako's story inspired her friends, who later raised money from around the world to build the Children's Peace Monument in Hiroshima Peace Park.

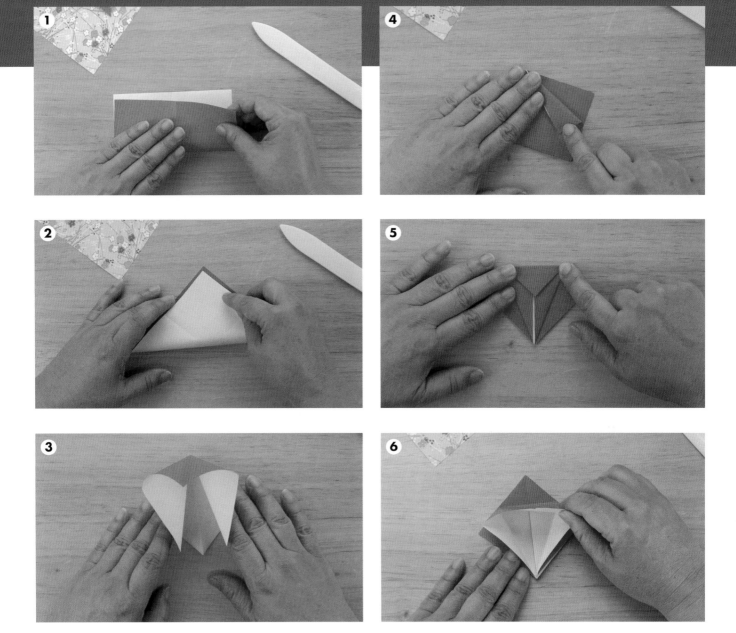

1. To fold the origami cranes, create guidelines by folding the origami paper in half, horizontally. Crease and open. Fold vertically, crease, and open.

2. Turn the paper a quarter turn and create two diagonal guidelines. Fold the bottom corner to the top corner, crease, and open. Turn the paper a quarter turn again and repeat. You should have four guidelines: two diagonally from corner to corner, one vertical, and one horizontal.

3. With the paper color-side down and the top and bottom corners aligned vertically, bend the top corner down toward the bottom corner. At the same time, press the side corners toward the bottom corner. Use the folded guidelines to help. Crease the paper on these guidelines. You have just created a diamond shape.

4. Next, create another set of guidelines. Orient the diamond shape with the opening facing up. Fold the right corner to the center with the edge aligned vertically along the center line. Repeat for the left side. Flip over and repeat for the back sections.

5. Turn the diamond shape so the opening is facing down. Fold the top corner so it meets the center line, using the horizontal top edges of the previous fold as your guide.

6. Unfold these three folds and gently pull the top layer upward, aiming the bottom corner away from you. Following the folded guidelines, you will crease the paper horizontally at the middle guideline.

(continued)

7 The edges will naturally come toward the center. Help the edge align vertically to the center line and crease the outer folds. You now have one tall narrow diamond shape with a symmetrical diamond shape underneath. Flip over and repeat so all are the same elongated diamond.

8 Make sure this elongated diamond shape has the divided sections pointing toward you. Fold the right corner of the diamond to the center mark, aligning the right outside edge with the center line. Repeat for the left side. Flip over and repeat.

9 Slightly separating the top and bottom folded edges on the right side, bring the right bottom point upward and inside the top and bottom flaps. You will naturally stop where this section splits. Crease at this intersection. This is called an inside reverse fold.

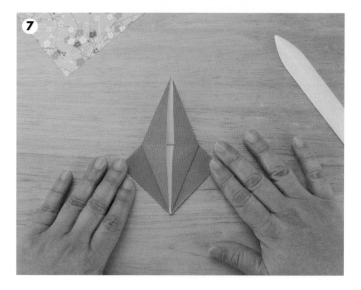

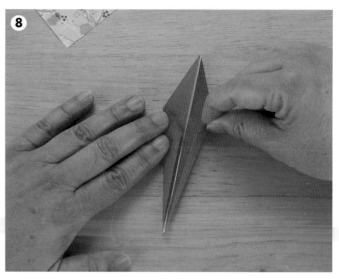

10 Repeat inside reverse fold for the left side.

11 Create another inside reverse fold about ¼ inch (6 mm) from the tip pointing down. This creates the head of the crane.

12 Fold the front top flap down. This is the wing. Congratulations! You've made your first Good Luck, Good Health, and Well Meaning Crane. Continue making two more. Trust me, they get easier as you make them.

13 Adhere the decorative paper to the folded card and adhere the cranes to the decorative paper, with the smallest crane toward the top of the page and the largest crane toward the bottom. This adds a sense of depth.

ORIGAMI WINGED HEART

A more modern adaptation of origami is a heart with wings, created by Francis Ow.

YOU WILL NEED

- 1 sheet red origami paper, 5 x 5 inches (12.5 x 12.5 cm)
- adhesive
- 1 sheet white embossed paper, 4½ x 4½ inches (11.4 x 11.4 cm)
- 1 red folded note card, 5½ x 5½ inches (14 x 14 cm)
- bone folder (optional)

1 To fold the heart, create a vertical and horizontal guideline by folding the origami paper in half vertically, then unfold and turn a quarter turn. Fold again in half, and your paper should have both guidelines.

2 Fold the bottom edge up to the horizontal guideline. Unfold. Repeat with the top edge, folding to the center guideline.

3 Flip over. Bring the upper-right corner to the center guide, aligning the top edge with the centered vertical guideline. Repeat with the upper-left corner. Your piece will look like a very wide house.

4 Fold the sides to the vertical center guideline. Unfold.

5 There is a little flap just below the top point where the opening is to the left. Tuck your finger inside the flap and push upward, bringing the left edge to align with the vertical center guideline. Repeat with the right side. You will have a rectangle.

(continued)

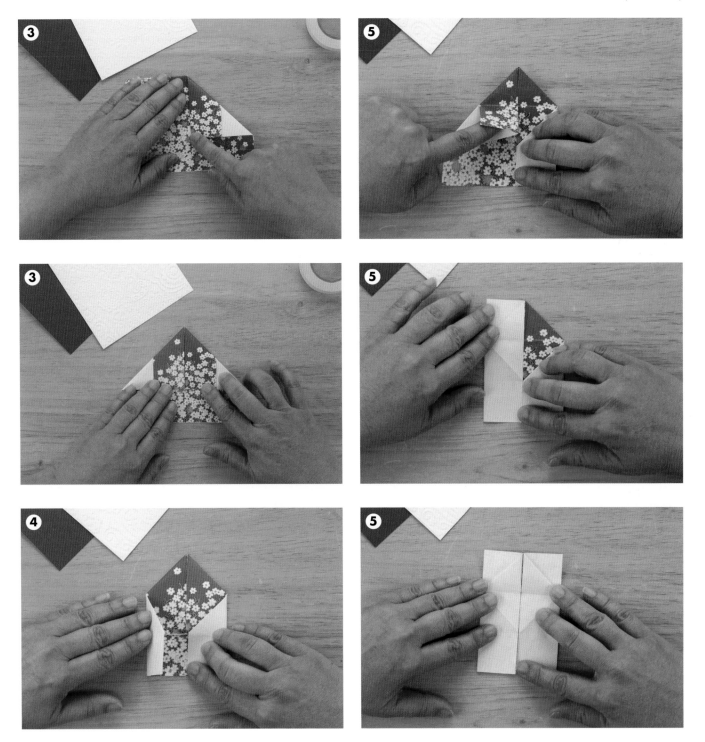

6 Opening the bottom two-thirds of the right flap, guide the left edge to the horizontal middle guideline of the diamond shape.

7 Align the bottom edge to the same horizontal guideline in the middle of the diamond. This will cause the left side to naturally mirror the right side fold. When finished, you will have an upside-down trapezoid or little boat.

8 Turn the piece upside down, and fold the outside bottom corners to the diagonal fold.

9 Fold the middle sections to the center guideline, creating two small upside-down pyramids.

10 Fold the tip of the pyramid to the edge of the two folded corners.

11 To create the wings, on the back, fold the pointed flap up. Flip over and turn the piece 180 degrees. Fold the little boat shape lengthwise (horizontally) in half, unfold, and fold in half again. Repeat one more time, creating eight guidelines. With this section unfolded, fold an accordion-style fold.

12 Pinch the center mark and unfold the outer sections (spreading the wings).

13 Adhere the embossed paper to the folded card and then adhere the origami winged heart.

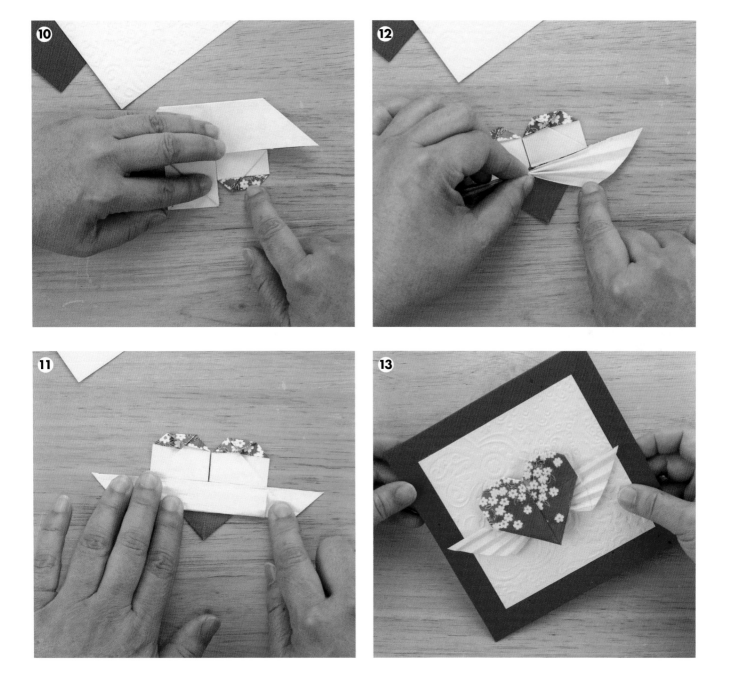

YOU WILL NEED

- 1 sheet white card stock
- adhesive
- 1 black folded note card, 1¼ x 5½ inches (3.2 x 14 cm)
- black marker (optional, if writing)
- scoring tool
- ruler
- penknife
- cutting mat
- bone folder

Pop-Up Cards

Pop-up cards are an adaption of "movable" or "pop-up" books. It is interesting that the beginning of movable books is credited to a Benedictine monk, Matthew Paris (c. 1200–1259), who attached volvelles (wheeled charts) to pages to help calculate holy dates. Several centuries later, the art of movable elements on book pages shifted from instructional tools for adults to entertainment for children. These books were scenes that "popped up" from the flat pages. The creation and introduction of pop-up books by Louis Giraud and Theodore Brown led to the use of pop-up techniques for greeting cards.

SINGLE-CUT HI

This easy and fast method for creating a pop-up card uses single cuts. Simple straight lines with strategically placed folds lift images from the flat surface of the card. The letters for "HI" are simple and illustrate the technique, but you can use any word to create the message you wish to send.

Some Things Remain the Same

When making this style of pop-up card, the distance of the raised (pop-up) feature is the same measurement below the center fold line and the measurement above the top of the raised feature. For this card, it is ½ inch (1.3 cm).

162   THE COMPLETE PHOTO GUIDE TO CARDMAKING

1 With the white cardstock oriented vertically, write or print the word "HI" near the center of the page. With a ruler, draw guidelines ½ inch (1.3 cm) from the top of the letters, at the tops of the letters, at the center of the page, and ½ inch (1.3 cm) below the center line.

2 Score the image at the guidelines you made in step 1.

3 Using a ruler and penknife on a cutting mat, cut lengthwise along the sides of the letters, starting at the mark ½ inch (1.3 cm) above the letters and ending ½ inch (1.3 cm) below the scored line for the center fold.

4 Push the letters forward, and carefully fold along the scored lines. Fold the top score line forward, the second score line (top of the letter) down, push the center scored mark back, and push the bottom of the letters forward.

5 Complete the fold by pressing together and creasing the scored lines.

6 Apply glue to the back of the top panel to adhere to the folded card. Be sure to glue to the side edges and sections between the letters, but be careful to keep the glue contained only on the back. Spilled glue can cause your card to stick to itself.

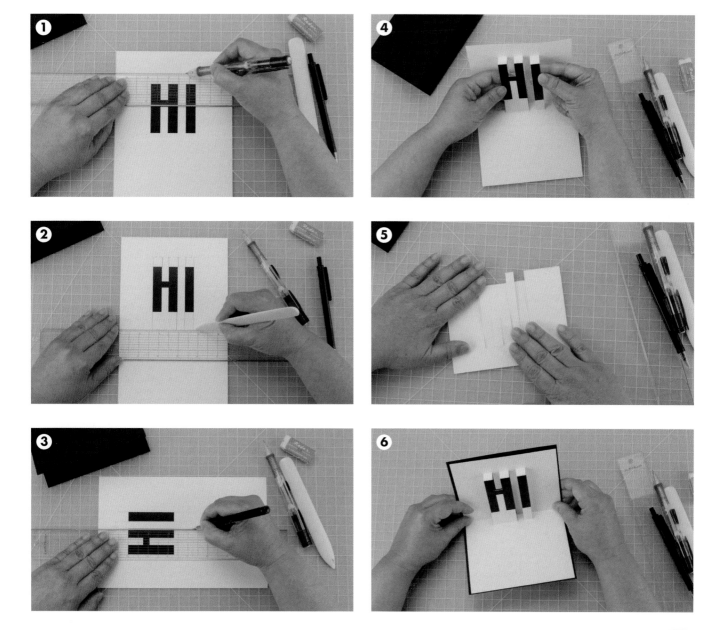

STACK OF BOXES

Everyone loves presents, especially ones that come in stacked boxes.
This pop-up element sends a whimsical yet special message.

YOU WILL NEED

- 3 pieces decorative card stock in graduating measurements, 3½ x 1½ inches, 2½ x 1¼ inches, and 2 x 1 inch (8.9 x 3.8 cm, 6.4 x 3.2 cm, and 5 x 2.5 cm)

- adhesive

- 3 pieces ¼-inch (6 mm) ribbon, 8 inches (20 cm), cut in half

- rhinestone-style embellishments

- 1 white folded note card, 4½ x 5½ inches (11.4 x 14 cm)

- 8 hinge-style adhesive pieces (a hinge is a rectangular piece of plastic divided into 2 equal squares with clear adhesive on one side)

- 3 artificial flowers (single layer) and broad petals, 1¼ inches (3.2 cm) diameter

- double-sided tape

- 1 sheet decorative card stock, 4 x 5¼ inches (10 x 13.4 cm)

- ruler

- pencil

- scissors

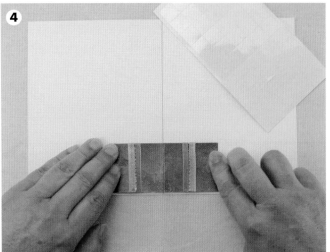

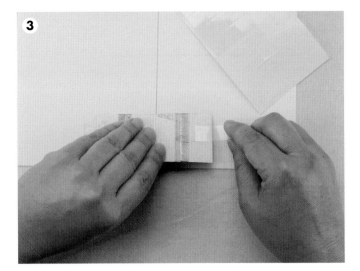

1 To make the faux stack of boxes, fold the decorative rectangular pieces in half. Glue the ribbon and rhinestone decorations vertically along the center mark on each half of the rectangles. Set aside.

2 With a ruler and pencil, draw a center guideline along the center fold of the note card to help align the gift box rectangles.

3 Position two of the clear adhesive hinges on the back of the largest rectangle along the side edges. Bend along the perforated line with the sticky sides out, and adhere one side up to the perforated line along the edge of the gift box rectangle. One section will be stuck to the paper and one section of the hinge will hang off the edge of the cutout.

4 Turn over the gift box rectangle and bend the hinge tabs toward the center fold on the rectangle and align the center folds. Press the rectangle and adhere to the base card approximately ⅛ inch (3 mm) from the bottom edge.

5 Repeat with the next two faux gift-box rectangles, graduating in size. Make sure the center folds align with the center fold of the card.

(continued)

6 Carefully fold the base card and help the faux gift boxes "pop up" if needed.

7 To add the floral top to the stack of gift boxes, apply a clear adhesive hinge to the right side of one flower, making sure half of the hinge overhangs to the outside of the petal. Repeat for a second flower. You should now have two silk flowers, each with a hinge that overhangs the petal. It is good to mentally label these as flower 1 and flower 2.

8 Fold flower 3 in half to establish the center of the flower. Lay flat on the table. Apply double-sided tape to the back.

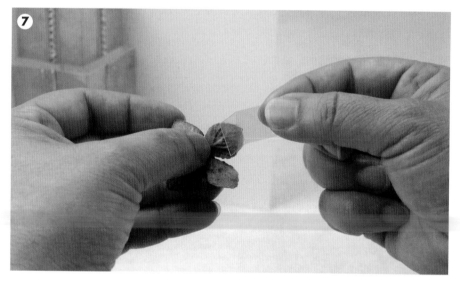

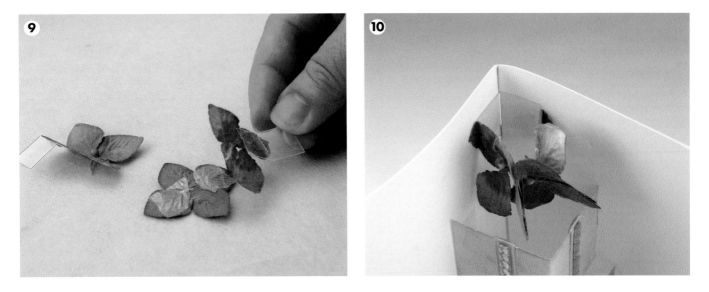

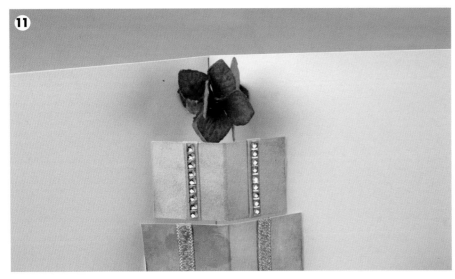

9 Align flower 1 above flower 3 and adhere the non adhesive petal to one side of flower 3. Repeat by adhering the non adhesive petal of flower 2 to the other side of flower 3.

10 Adhere the exposed adhesive on the hinge to the folded card with the edge of the hinge aligned with the center fold. Manipulate the second hinge and align with the attached hinge and secure along the center fold.

11 Carefully pull the flower out so it pops up along with the gift boxes.

12 Adhere the decorative card stock to the front of the card.

YOU WILL NEED

- 2 sheets clear plastic, 4 x 4 inches (10 x 10 cm)
- clear double-sided tape
- 2 rocket images (it's best if the image is symmetrical)
- 1 white folded note card, 4¼ x 5½ inches (10.8 x 14 cm)
- 1 sheet white vellum (officially called clear vellum)
- permanent ink pen
- scissors

UP IN THE AIR ROCKET

A spiral cut from clear plastic cleverly creates the mechanism to make this little rocket pop-up so it looks like it's flying.

1 Draw a 3½- to 4-inch (8.9 to 10 cm) spiral on the clear plastic with a fine line permanent pen and cut both sheets of the clear plastic as if it were one sheet. You should have duplicate clear spirals.

2 Adhere the outer points of the spiral together with double-sided tape.

(continued)

Clean Up Mistakes

There are times when I make a mistake on the clear plastic and have no way to erase it. A paper towel dipped in rubbing alcohol is a great permanent-ink eraser.

Perfect Alignment, or
What Appears to Be Perfect

When hand cutting two identical pieces to mirror and adhere together, it is difficult to cut and align with precision. If you outline the edge of the cutout shape with a matching color marker and also color the back about 1/8 to 1/4 inch (3 to 6 mm) from the edge, when glued together, your piece will appear to be cut precisely.

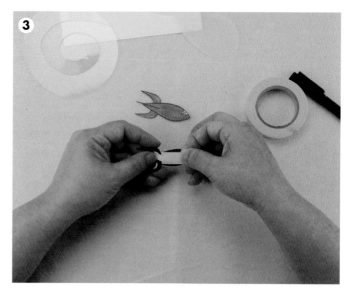

3 Place a piece of double-sided tape on the backs of both rockets and adhere the first rocket to the outer tip of the spiral. Adhere the second rocket by aligning and matching the first one.

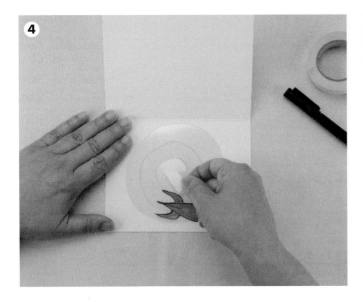

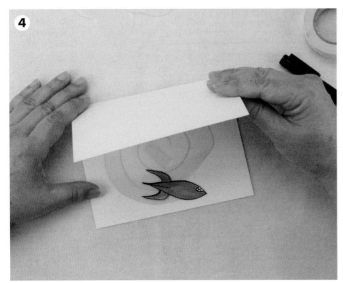

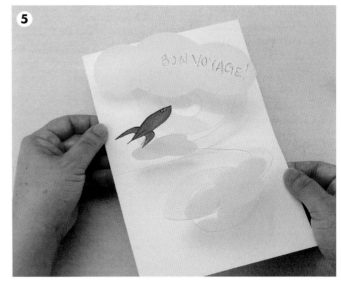

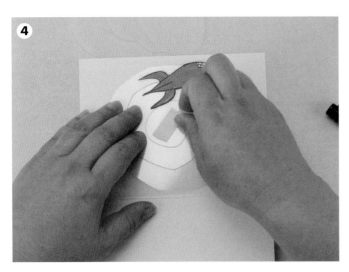

4 Position the spiral within the folded card with the rocket pointing toward the opening of the card. Place a piece of double-sided tape on the top spiral at the center point. Close the card. This will stick the top of the card to one side of the spiral. Turn over the card and repeat for the bottom panel.

5 Cut out clouds from the vellum and adhere to the spiral in a couple of places, first double-checking that they do not stick out beyond the edges of the folded card.

Gift or Money Cards

Buying gifts for my Generation XYZ family and friends can be difficult. They either already have it, don't like what I've picked out, or grew 3 inches (7.5 cm) taller in the meantime. So giving gift cards (and sometimes money) is a nice solution, but often these types of gifts seem a little impersonal. Creating the card that holds the gift card makes everything fun and personal.

HIP POCKET

When a greeting card is not quite enough, adding a pocket can turn it into a surprise gift. This image of a pair of jeans is a great method for a gift card delivery.

YOU WILL NEED

- 1 image jeans with back pocket
- ⅜-inch (1 cm)-wide decorative trim, 6 inches (15 cm)
- adhesive
- 1 folded note card, 4¼ x 5½ inches (10.8 x 14 cm)
- ruler
- penknife
- cutting mat
- hole punch, 1/16 inch (1.5 mm)
- scissors

1 With a ruler and penknife on a cutting mat, cut a slit along the top of the pocket.

2 Cut ½-inch (1.3 cm) slices along the sides of the belt loops.

3 Trim the top area of the jeans.

4 Thread the decorative trim through the belt loops, fold over and secure to the back of the card with adhesive.

5 Adhere the jeans to the folded card. Apply the adhesive along the edges of the jeans image and a small amount just under the pocket image. This will help keep the gift card from completely sliding under the pocket opening.

6 Insert the gift card into the pocket.

Add Strength with a Teeny Punched Hole

I suppose if we ask Mr. Physics, we could get an answer as to why a teeny punched hole at the ends of a cut line helps prevent the cut line from tearing.

YOU WILL NEED

- 1 sheet decorative paper, 2½ x 2½ inches (6.4 x 6.4 cm)

- adhesive

- 1 mini folded square note card, 3 x 3 inches (7.5 x 7.5 cm)

- 1 sheet decorative card stock, 5¼ x 5¼ inches (13.4 x 13.4 cm)

- 1 folded note card, 5½ x 5½ inches (14 x 14 cm)

- 1 sheet white (clear) vellum, 5½ x 8½ inches (14 x 21.6 cm)

- glue

- 1 tassel with sliding closure

- purchased mini envelope template or pattern on page 249

- pencil

- scoring tool

- scissors

- bone folder

MINI ENVELOPE CARD

Miniature objects are really cute, but they also add a unique dimension to this style card. To make the mini envelope for the center of this card, you can purchase a plastic template or trace the pattern provided on page 249.

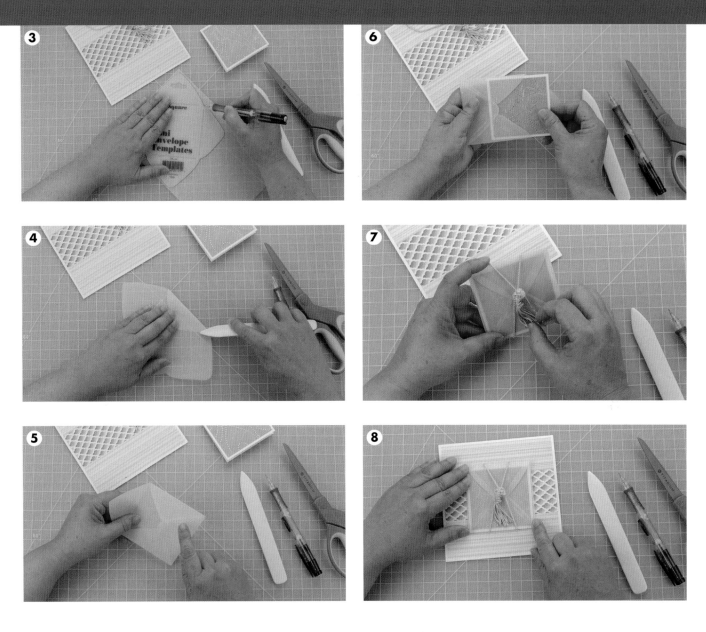

1 Make the mini folded card by adhering the decorative 2½ x 2½-inch (6.4 x 6.4 cm) piece to the front of the folded 3 x 3-inch (7.5 x 7.5 cm) card. Set aside.

2 Adhere the decorative 5¼ x 5¼-inch (13.4 x 13.4 cm) sheet to the 5½ x 5½-inch (14 x 14 cm) folded card. Set aside.

3 Make the mini envelope from the vellum using the mini envelope template (page 249). Trace the outline of the template with a pencil. Score within the slots for folding.

4 Cut out the shape and fold along the scored lines.

5 Apply adhesive to the areas of the flaps where they overlap. If necessary, use the bone folder or pencil to mark this area. Be careful not to have glue spill over to the inside of the envelope.

6 Insert the mini square card into the mini square envelope. Close the top flap.

7 With the fringe of the tassel hanging down and placed near the point of the flap, wrap the loop of the tassel around the back of the envelope and bring it from the back to the front. Hook the little sliding ball with the loop of the tassel to close the envelope.

8 Adhere the mini envelope to the front of the card.

GIFT CARD WALLET

Can't decide on which gift card to give? This little paper wallet will help present several gift cards at once. The envelopes are made to match, and adhering them to the accordion fold brings these little pockets to life.

YOU WILL NEED

- 3 sheets complementary decorative paper, 6 x 6 inches (15.2 x 15.2 cm)
- glue
- 6 decorative buttons
- 1 sheet matching decorative card stock, 6 x 12 inches (15.2 x 30.5 cm)
- 1 sheet decorative card stock, 12 x 12 inches (30.5 x 30.5 cm)
- 1 elastic ponytail holder
- purchased gift card envelope template or pattern on page 249
- ruler
- scoring tool
- scissors
- bone folder

1 Make 3 gift card envelopes from the template using 3 variations of decorative 6 x 6 inches (15.2 x 15.2 cm) paper. Adhere 1 button to each flap. Set aside.

2 With the 6 x 12-inch (15.2 x 30.5 cm) card stock positioned horizontally, measure and vertically score at the 4- and 8-inch (10 and 20.3 cm) marks. Set aside.

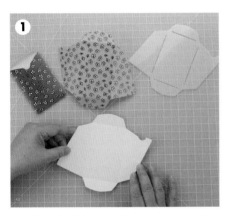

3 Cut the 12 x 12-inch (30.5 x 30.5 cm) sheet into the following pieces: 5¾ x 12 inches, 5½ x 3½ inches (set this one aside), and 1 x 12 inches (14.6 x 30.5 cm, 14 x 8.9 cm, and 2.5 x 30.5 cm).

4 Position the 5¾ x 12-inch (14.6 x 30.5 cm) sheet horizontally on your work surface. Using a bone folder and ruler or scoring board, vertically mark the following panels: 3⅞ inches (9.8 cm), six ½-inch (1.3 cm) segments, 3⅞ inches (9.8 cm), and 1¼ inches (3.2 cm).

5 Fold the scored lines at the ½-inch (1.3 cm) segments to create accordion folds. There should be three mountains.

6 Lay the 6 x 12-inch (15.2 x 30.5 cm) sheet face down in front of you. Apply glue to the right panel of the accordion-folded card and adhere to

the 4-inch (10 cm) side of the 6 x 12-inch (15.2 x 30.5 cm) sheet.

7 Apply glue to the left panel of the accordion-folded card and adhere to the middle panel of the 6 x 12-inch (15.2 x 30.5 cm) sheet. The accordion-folded section in the middle will not be attached but should be standing.

8 Glue the gift card envelopes to the valleys of the accordion folds, positioning them across the width of the card.

9 Glue 5½ x 3½-inch sheet to the blank panel.

10 Glue the remaining three buttons to the front panel of the folded card. Wrap the 1-inch (2.5 cm)-wide strip around the wallet and secure with the elastic ponytail holder. Be sure to insert the gift cards into the gift card envelopes before sending this card.

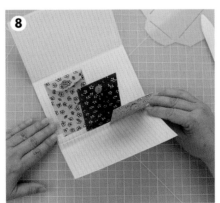

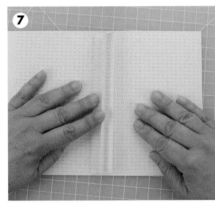

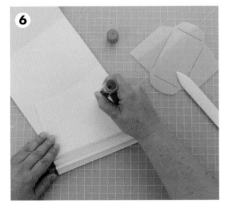

YOU WILL NEED

- 1 red envelope, 4 x 9 inches (10 x 22.9 cm)
- 1 sheet gold card stock, 2½ x 11 inches (6.4 x 28 cm)
- 1-inch (2.5 cm) wide red chiffon ribbon, 15 inches (38 cm)
- embossing folder and embossing machine
- scissors
- ruler
- pencil
- scoring tool
- bone folder
- hole punch, 1/16 inch (1.5 mm) (optional)

Continue the Pattern

If the embossing folder is smaller than the paper, you can flip it and continue the pattern.

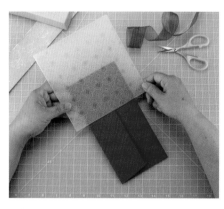

RED ENVELOPE

You can never have enough good luck, and receiving a red envelope is good. In China, these red envelopes are usually used for holidays and special occasions and generally hold a little money. It is a tradition where married couples give to single people but mostly to children. Who wouldn't be happy receiving a red envelope?

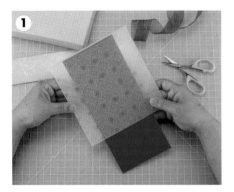

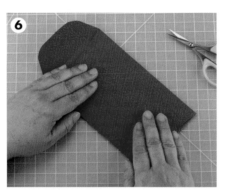

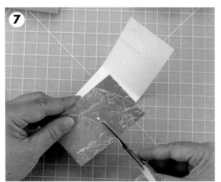

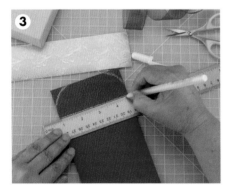

1 Emboss the plain red envelope with an embossing folder in an embossing machine.

2 To modify this envelope to open vertically, trim 1 inch (2.5 cm) off one end of the envelope.

3 Turn the envelope vertically. With a ruler and pencil, draw a horizontal scoring guideline 1 inch (2.5 cm) below the edge of the envelope. Draw two quarter circles to round the corners of the envelope flap.

4 On the back of the envelope, draw two guidelines from the horizontal scored line, angling to the center and ½ inch (1.3 cm) lower.

5 Open the flap of the envelope and trim along the angled guides.

6 Seal the envelope flap (which is now the center seam).

7 Create a band with the gold-colored card stock by wrapping the band around the envelope. It will fold approximately in thirds. Mark the center of the folded band, and punch a small hole in the left section. Using this hole as a guide, punch the right section at the center mark. Cut the left section of the band upward to the center mark. Cut the right section of the band from the top edge downward to the center mark.

8 Insert the downward slice into the upward slice, connecting the two sections of the band. Slide onto the envelope, closing the envelope flap.

9 Tie the ribbon around the band to decorate.

Blocks of Color

This style of card is surprisingly easy. The best part is you can complete several cards at one time by assembling these scraps of paper. We can all use that little bit of extra time saved from the efficiency of making these cards.

MIX IT UP

Cut it up, mix and match, and you have the beginning for two cards at one time.

YOU WILL NEED

- 2 sheets decorative paper, 4¼ x 5½ inches (10.8 x 14 cm), in two different colors

- 2-inch (5 cm)-wide double-sided tape

- 1 butterfly image

- 1 folded note card, 4¼ x 5½ inches (10.8 x 14 cm) (a second one is needed if you want to make 2 cards at the same time)

- paper trimmer

- chisel-tip gold metallic marker

1 Cut the two decorative sheets in half horizontally and vertically.

2 Using two pieces of each color, arrange them in alternating colors.

3 Using a 6-inch (15.2 cm) strip of double-sided tape, position the sticky side up and vertically apply one of each quartered piece of paper in opposing colors to the tape. Align the pieces along the horizontal center line.

4 Continue with the second pair of pieces. Be sure to carefully align along the center vertical and horizontal lines. It is okay to leave the outside edges uneven because the next step is to trim the edges square.

5 Crop the butterfly image to 3¼ x 2¾ inches (8.3 x 7 cm). Apply a thin line of metallic ink to the edges of the image.

6 Adhere the butterfly to the quartered pieces and adhere to the folded card.

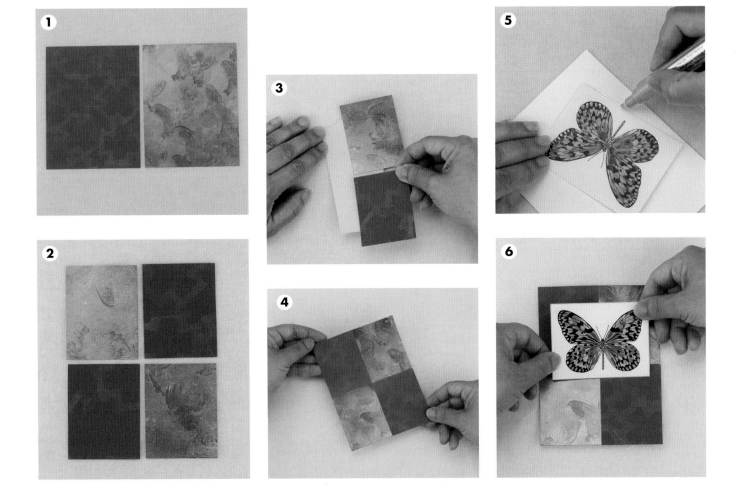

No Need for Rulers

Many people think I use a ruler to draw the straight metallic lines around the edges of the card. But when they see no ruler they think I'm really skilled. The secret is to gently push the tip of the pen toward the card while guiding it along the edge. If you push too hard you may jump over the edge. Practice—it really works.

YOU WILL NEED

- 2 sheets matching decorative card stock, 4¼ x 5½ inches (10.8 x 14 cm), one in red and one in white

- masking tape

- 2-inch (5 cm)-wide double-sided tape

- 1 Twinchie (thick and sturdy card stock), 2 x 2 inches (5 x 5 cm)

- 1 white folded note card, 4¼ x 5½ inches (10.8 x 14 cm)

- ruler

- penknife

- cutting mat

- paper trimmer

PUZZLE IT TOGETHER

Based on the same technique for the previous Mix It Up card, this one looks similar but needs just a little more attention. The patterned paper aligns perfectly, creating the illusion of clear colored overlays.

1 With a ruler and penknife on a cutting mat, cut the red decorative card stock in half vertically.

2 Align one half on top of the white decorative card stock, matching the design. This will be the guide to cut the second decorative card stock in half.

3 Secure with masking tape so the papers do not slip.

4 Align the ruler along the edge of the half sheet and cut the bottom paper in half.

(continued)

5 You will now have four half pieces.

6 Cut one of the half pieces in half again. This will be the guide to cut the second piece in half again. Lay it on top of the second half piece, and align the ruler along the edge. Cut in half again, creating a quarter sheet.

7 Continue cutting each piece until there are eight sections.

8 Rearrange the sections.

9 Assemble the sections. Place each section onto the sticky side of a 5-inch (12.5 cm) strip of double-sided tape. Make sure the design aligns along the center lines. The outside edges may be uneven but you will trim these away.

10 Square up the outside edges.

11 Adhere the Twinchie to the black-and-white printed paper, trim and color in. Match the pattern of the decorated card.

12 Adhere to the folded card to complete.

BARGELLO-STYLE PAPER QUILTING

This style of needlework found on chairs in the Bargello Palace in Florence inspired quilters to create beautiful patterns with pieces of fabric instead of threads. MaryJo McGraw creatively modified these techniques using paper instead of fabric. After sharing her technique, she inspired me to make these beautiful yet practical cards. Using scraps of paper, you can turn leftovers into a visual feast.

YOU WILL NEED

- 2 sheets decorative paper, one 3¾ x 5 inches (9.5 x 12.5 cm) and one 5 x 6 inches (12.5 x 15.2 cm)

- 1 sheet contrasting decorative paper, 5 x 6 inches (12.5 x 15.2 cm)

- 2 adhesive mailing labels, 2 x 4 inches (5 x 10 cm), or 2-inch (5 cm)-wide double-sided tape

- adhesive

- 1 sheet dark brown card stock, 2¼ x 4¼ inches (5.7 x 10.8 cm)

- 1 white folded note card, 4¼ x 5½ inches (10.8 x 14 cm)

- paper trimmer

1. Set aside the 3¾ x 5-inch (9.5 x 12.5 cm) sheet of decorative paper. Cut at least two ½-inch (1.3 cm) strips from the remaining sheet of decorative paper and from the contrasting paper. Make sure the strips are long enough to cover the mailing label lengthwise.

2. Peel off one label and lay it sticky side up on the table in front of you.

3. Apply each color strip in alternating colors to the label. Align vertically using the edge as a guide. Adhere the next piece, leaving no space between strips.

4. Trim the edges flush with the paper trimmer, and cut into four 1 x 2-inch (2.5 x 5 cm) pieces.

5. Place the second mailing label on the table vertically and sticky side up. Align the first 1 x 2-inch (2.5 x 5 cm) piece with the top edge of the label. Apply the second piece, but turn it 180 degrees. The color pattern will be inverted and when continued will create a checkerboard pattern.

6. Adhere to the brown card stock to create a frame, then adhere to the 3¾ x 5-inch (9.5 x 12.5 cm) sheet of decorative paper. Finally, adhere to the folded card.

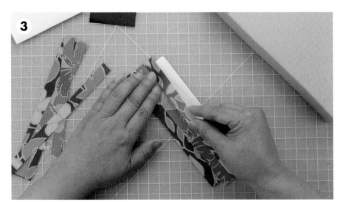

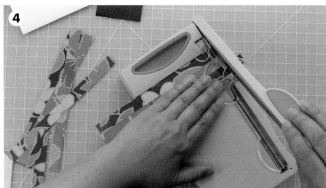

YOU WILL NEED

- 4 strips double-sided tape, 2 x 6 inches (5 x 15.2 cm)
- 15 strips pink decorative paper, ¼ x at least 4 inches (6 mm x 10 cm)
- 15 strips blue decorative paper, ¼ x at least 4 inches (6 mm x 10 cm)
- 1 sheet dark brown card stock, 5½ x 2¼ inches (15 x 5.7 cm)
- 1½-inch (3.8 cm)-wide dark brown ribbon, 15 inches (38.1 cm)
- 1 folded note card, 5½ x 4¼ inches (14 x 10.8 cm)
- cutting mat with grid and diagonal guidelines
- scissors
- ruler
- penknife

PAPER MOSAIC CHEVRONS

Modifying this technique creates a vast arrangement of patterns. If you are good at puzzles, the possibilities will keep you busy until you have used up all the leftover strips of paper you've been saving.

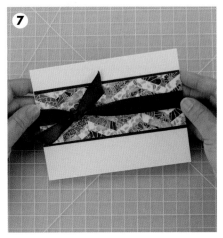

1 Secure the double-sided tape to the cutting mat. Trim a small section of the release paper from the back of the tape.

2 Align one strip of tape along the 45-degree diagonal guideline and stick to the mat.

3 Using the horizontal guidelines on the mat, alternately adhere the pink and blue strips to the sticky tape, leaving no space between strips. Trim the excess from the edges of the tape.

4 Repeat with another strip of tape, positioning the tape on the opposite diagonal guideline.

5 With a ruler and penknife, cut these two pieces in half, lengthwise. You should have four 1-inch (2.5 cm) strips.

6 Adhere the third strip of double-sided tape horizontally to the cutting mat. Peel off the release paper from one 1-inch (2.5 cm) strip and apply to the left side of the tape. Continue alternating diagonal patterns, creating a zigzag, or chevron, pattern. Trim. Using the bottom half of the strips, continue the pattern. Crop all rough edges.

7 Adhere to the 5½-inch (14 cm) band of card stock. Wrap the ribbon around the band and tie a granny knot. Adhere to the folded card with the remaining piece of double-sided tape.

INTRIGUING GEOMETRIC

The technique of marquetry can be as complicated or as simple as you wish. Sometimes, the cleaner the lines, the more elegant it appears.

Marquetry or Wood Veneer Inlay

Inlaid-wood decoration has been a beautiful art form for centuries. I first saw this in an award plaque handmade by a favorite university professor. Getting one of Jack's handmade plaques was really special. When asked how it was made, he said it was a secret with a wide smile and a twinkle in his eye. It wasn't until after I graduated that he finally taught me how to make these plaques. The technique is similar for this card but made incredibly easy with the improvement of veneer manufacturing. Today, these veneers are paper thin and can be easily cut with scissors, craft knives, and die-cutting machines.

YOU WILL NEED

- 1 geometric pattern
- 3 half sheets printable wood veneer in different colors
- low-tack masking tape
- 2-inch (5 cm)-wide double-sided tape
- 1 sheet card stock in a color matching the veneer, 3¼ x 4¼ inches (8.3 x 10.8 cm)
- 1 plum-colored folded note card, 5½ x 5½ inches (14 x 14 cm)
- 2 sheets card stock, 3¼ x 4¼ inches (8.3 x 10.8 cm)
- 2 additional folded cards in any color or size that will frame 3¼ x 4¼ inches (8.3 x 10.8 cm)
- penknife
- ruler
- cutting mat
- scissors

1. Print a geometric pattern on the back of each of the three sheets of printable wood veneer. For this card, the pattern is five connected, elongated diamonds cut in half. Using a ruler and penknife on a cutting mat, cut out the pattern on all three sheets.

2. Apply a strip of masking tape to the back of the cutout shapes to help keep the pieces together.

3. Lay a 5-inch (12.5 cm) strip of the 2-inch (5 cm) double-sided tape, sticky side up, on the table in front of you. Carefully remove the top piece from one color wood and lightly tack it to the top area of the tape. From the second colored-wood cutouts, carefully remove the left piece from the elongated diamonds, and position on the double-sided tape, reassembling the puzzle. Take the right side of the elongated diamond from the third color of wood and carefully place on the double-sided tape. Continue filling in the pattern.

4. You will need to add a little extra double-sided tape to the bottom of the pattern to adhere the bottom piece.

5. Trim away the exposed double-sided tape.

6. Adhere to the 3¼ x 4¼-inch (8.3 x 10.8 cm) card stock and adhere to the folded card. The remaining pieces will make two additional cards.

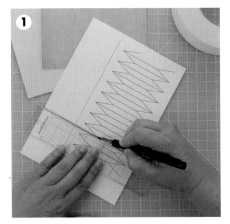

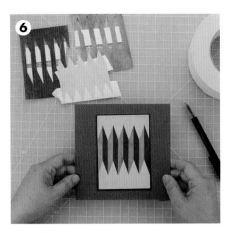

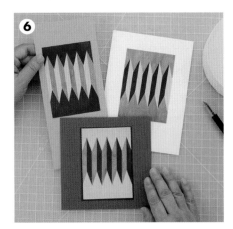

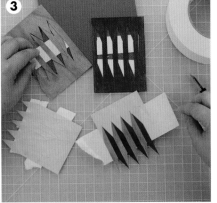

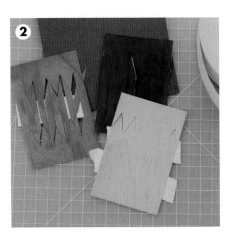

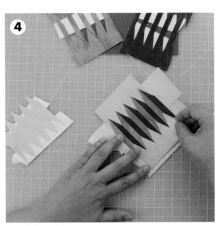

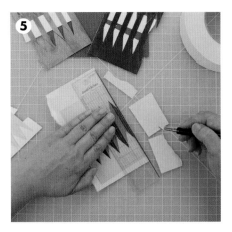

- 1 folded note card, 4¼ x 5½ inches (10.8 x 14 cm)
- 1 sheet card stock, 4⅛ x 5⅜ inches (10.5 x 13.7 cm)
- double-sided tape
- 1 sheet window plastic, 4¼ x 5½ inches (10.8 x 14 cm)
- 1 sheet decorative card stock, 4 x 5¼ inches (10 x 13.4 cm)
- 1 butterfly image
- ruler
- penknife
- cutting mat
- pencil

Window Cards

A different way to create a framed effect for a card, this clear sheet of plastic gives the illusion you are looking through glass. Be creative— so many big windows with gorgeous views to enjoy.

FLOATING IMAGE

The butterfly on this window card appears to be floating, an optical illusion easily re-created with a clear sheet of window plastic.

Fractions Do Not Have to Be Scary

I've included dimensions in fractions that are sometimes in ⅛-inch (3 mm) increments. This is only because the frame should be slightly smaller than the card frame. It is to cover up the messy-looking adhesive on the back of the front panel.

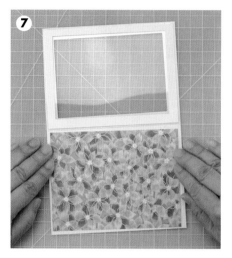

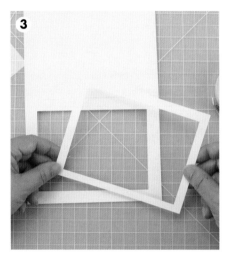

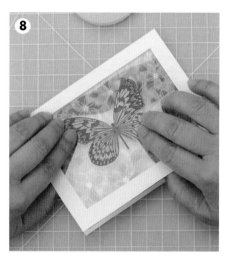

1 Cut a frame in one panel of the folded card using a ruler and penknife on a cutting mat. Align the bottom edge of the card with the ½-inch (1.3 cm) horizontal line on the ruler. Cut from the left ½-inch (1.3 cm) vertical mark to the right ½-inch (1.3 cm) vertical mark.

2 Turn the card a quarter turn and cut a ½-inch (1.3 cm) margin. Repeat to complete the frame.

3 Cut a separate frame from the 4⅛ x 5⅜-inch (10.5 x 13.7 cm) sheet of card stock. Cut an inside opening slightly larger than the opening of the card frame, 3⅝ x 4⅞ inches (9.2 x 12.4 cm).

4 Assemble the card by applying the double-sided tape to the inside of the frame panel.

5 Apply the window plastic to the adhesive.

6 Layer on the separate frame to cover the tape marks.

7 Apply the decorative paper to the back panel of the card.

8 Using the double-sided tape, adhere the cutout butterfly to the front of the card on the window plastic.

FOREGROUND IN FOCUS

This card makes you feel like you are swimming among the sea life.
Very pretty and you don't get wet.

YOU WILL NEED

- 1 kraft-colored folded note card, 5 x 7 inches (12.5 x 17.8 cm)
- 1 sheet window plastic, 4¼ x 5½ inches (10.8 x 14 cm)
- double-sided tape
- tassel embellishment
- rubber stamps of shell, starfish, and coral
- ink pads
- markers
- pencil
- steel-edge ruler
- penknife
- cutting mat

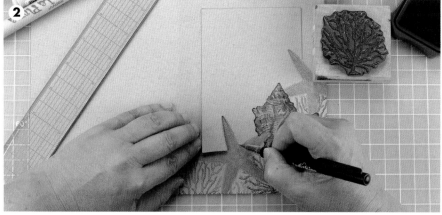

1 Rubber stamp the shell, starfish, and coral in the bottom-right corner on the front of the card. Color images with markers. Draw a ¾-inch (2 cm) frame on the front panel with a pencil and ruler. Note where the guideline intersects with the stamped image.

2 Starting at the top of the stamped image on the left side edge, use the penknife and a cutting mat to cut around the outline of the stamped images, stopping ¾ inch (2 cm) from the left and right edges. Starting at the right side, use the ruler to help cut the straight line ¾ inch (2 cm) from the right side edge, stopping ¾ inch (2 cm) from the top. Repeat for the top and left sides. You should now have a ¾-inch frame at the left, top, and right sides of the card, with the shells cut out in the bottom right corner.

3 Using the window as your guideline, stamp the coral inside the card on the right panel. Make sure you can see some of the image when the card is closed.

4 Adhere the window plastic to the inside of the front cutout panel with double-sided tape. Add tassel embellishment.

YOU WILL NEED

- 1 sheet vellum, 4¼ x 5½ inches (10.8 x 14 cm)
- adhesive
- 1 sheet red card stock, 3 x 2¼ inches (7.5 x 5.7 cm)
- 1 sheet white card stock, 3¼ x 2½ inches (7.8 x 6.4 cm)
- 1 pink folded card, 4¼ x 5½ inches (10.8 x 14 cm)
- pattern or rubber stamp
- white ink and dip pen, or white marking pen, or rubber stamp and white ink pad
- burnishing tool
- foam mat
- pricking tool
- permanent ink pens or oil-based crayons

Parchment Craft

This art form was created in the sixteenth century by monks and nuns, who discovered beautiful results from embossing and pricking the parchment or vellum (pages made from animal skins) that they used to handwrite religious documents. Primarily practiced by Catholic artisans, the craft migrated from Europe to South America, although it did not become popular until the mid-1950s, when it was reintroduced with newer and easier-to-use synthetic parchment.

APPLYING THE PATTERN

Originally, patterns were traced with white ink and mapping (dip) pens. Today, there are many other options, including opaque white marking pens and rubber stamps with white ink.

1 Trace the pattern onto the sheet of vellum in white ink or stamp the image. Let dry.

2 Burnish within the open areas of the design.

3 On a foam mat, prick the outside lines and tear or cut along the pricked dotted lines.

4 On the back, color with permanent inks or oil-based crayons.

5 Adhere to the red card stock, then adhere to the white card stock, then adhere to the folded card.

COLORED VELLUM

Originally, parchment craft was done on white-colored vellum. Today, paper manufacturers have created a variety of colored vellums, which add ambience to your card creations.

YOU WILL NEED

- white ink pad
- 1 sheet goldenrod vellum, 4¼ x 5½ inches (10.8 x 14 cm)
- 1 sheet mustard card stock, 3½ x 5½ inches (8.9 x 14 cm)
- double-sided tape
- 1 cream-colored folded note card, 5½ x 5½ inches (14 x 14 cm)
- butterfly image (optional)
- rubber stamp of flowers (outline with line weight heavier than 1 mm)
- burnishing tool
- foam mat
- pricking tool
- ruler
- craft knife or paper cutter
- scissors

1 Stamp the image with white ink onto the vellum. Let dry.

2 Burnish along the image's lines and within the design.

3 Place on a foam mat and prick around the image, if desired.

4 Crop with a ruler and craft knife and adhere to the mustard-colored card stock, and then adhere to the folded card. Add a little dimension with a butterfly cutout, if desired.

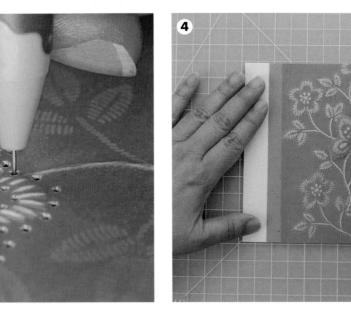

FAUX PARCHMENT CRAFT

If you like the look of parchment craft but you are in a hurry (not to mention, you suspect the recipient will not appreciate the work you've done—yes, there are a few who will think you just casually bought a card), a rubber stamp with white embossing powder is a quick solution.

YOU WILL NEED

- 1 sheet vellum, 5½ x 8½ inches (14 x 21.6 cm)
- pigment or embossing ink pad
- embossing powder, opaque white
- 1 sheet glitter paper, 4¼ x 5½ inches (10.8 x 14 cm)
- double-sided tape
- 3 pressed lavender flowers
- ½-inch (1.3 cm)-wide ribbon, 12 inches (30.5 cm)
- 1 folded colored note card, 5½ x 5½ inches (14 x 14 cm)
- rubber stamp of lace doily
- heat tool
- paper trimmer
- hot glue
- scissors

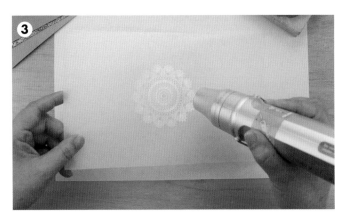

1 Stamp the lace doily image in the center of the vellum with pigment or embossing ink.

2 Pour the opaque white embossing powder over the image. The powder will stick to the wet ink. Shake off the excess powder and pour back into the container.

3 Melt the powder with the heat tool. Be careful not to overheat the powder or it can scorch. Stamp the lace doily on either side of the first image. Repeat with the embossing powder.

4 Crop so the doily images are centered horizontally and the vellum measures 3¾ x 5 inches (9.5 x 12.5 cm). Adhere to the glitter paper with double-sided tape.

5 Adhere the lavender flowers to the vellum layer with hot glue. Wrap and tie the ribbon approximately 2 inches (5 cm) from the bottom and trim the ends.

6 Adhere the entire piece to the folded note card.

Hide the Adhesive

If you apply the adhesive on vellum or clear plastic, you will see the adhesive. But if you apply the adhesive underneath the stamped image, the adhesive is hidden.

YOU WILL NEED

- permanent ink pad
- 1 piece copper,
  2½ x 2½ inches
  (6.4 x 6.4 cm)
- 1 sheet black card stock,
  4½ x 4½ inches
  (10.8 x 10.8 cm)
- 1 clay-colored folded card,
  5½ x 5½ inches
  (14 x 14 cm)
- adhesive
- mica tiles
- rubber stamp of ivy leaf
- foam pad
- metal-embossing tools

Embossing

Many styles and techniques for cardmaking are representations of different methods used to create adornments for the decorative arts, from details on furniture to ornaments on buildings. One style of decoration commonly found is carved or embossed works. The skill required to make these carvings in stone, metal, bone, shell, or wood is labor intensive. With the innovation of technology, synthetic materials, and modified tools, the methods to copy this handiwork have given cardmakers the ability to create cards that imply importance and luxury.

METAL REPOUSSÉ

Handworked metal is how these beautiful embossed decorations are created. Simply trace the image with a stylus tool on one side of the metal and refine the image on the opposite side.

Not Enough Mica?

If the mica tiles are thick, you can peel layers apart, creating additional mica tiles. Even though these could be considered rocks, they can be cut into smaller pieces with a normal pair of scissors.

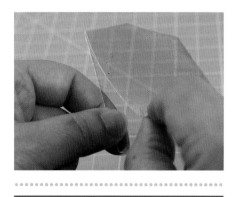

1. Rubber stamp the image onto the copper. This will be the back of the image. Working on the foam pad, use the stylus tool to trace the ivy design, creating an indentation in the metal.

2. Turn the copper over and, using the refining tool, press against the embossed image at the base of the shoulder to define the lines of the image.

3. Use the rotary decorative wheel to outline the image with dotted lines.

4. Assemble the card by adhering the black card stock to the clay-colored folded card. Arrange the mica tiles to cover most of the black card stock and adhere.

5. Adhere the embossed copper piece.

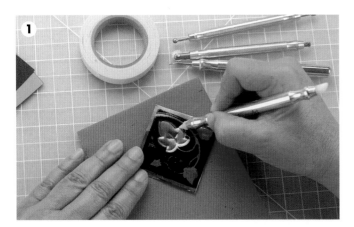

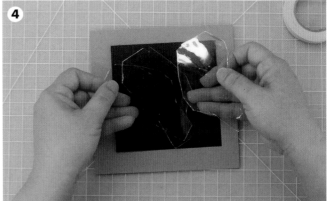

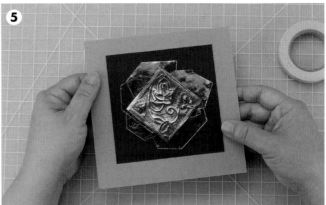

PRESSED PAPER EMBOSSING

Metal stencils are great for pressing the design into the paper, creating a relief. A little handwork is needed, but the beauty in its simplicity is impressive.

YOU WILL NEED

- 1 folded note card, 5 x 7 inches (12.5 x 17.8 cm)
- masking tape
- 1 metal stencil
- light table
- burnishing tool
- wax paper
- adhesive
- paper trimmer

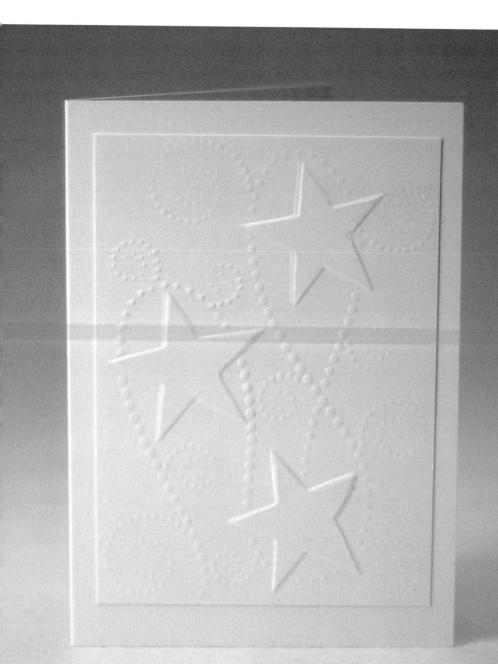

Short-Cut Light Source

If you are working on a small area, holding the stencil and paper combination against a window works well. Be sure not to push too hard.

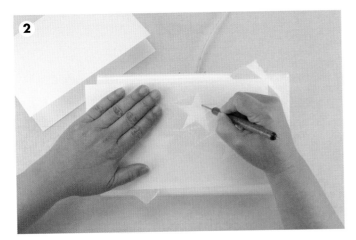

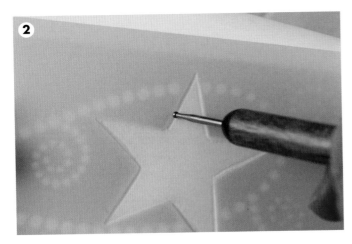

1 Position the stencil over a light table on the wax paper that is layered over the back of the card stock. Secure with masking tape.

2 Trace the image with the burnishing tool, pressing the inside edge of the stencil onto the paper.

3 Remove the stencil and turn the card over. The image will be raised and will appear to pop off the paper.

4 Crop using a paper trimmer and glue onto the folded card.

YOU WILL NEED

- 1 sheet card stock, 5½ x 8½ inches (14 x 21.6 cm)
- 1 sheet card stock with a greeting printed on it horizontally, 4¼ x 5½ inches (10.8 x 14 cm)
- self-adhesive foam squares
- 1 folded note card, 5½ x 5½ inches (14 x 14 cm)
- adhesive
- self-adhesive pearl embellishments
- embossing folder
- die-cutting machine
- ruler
- penknife
- cutting mat
- thin flourished cutting die
- wax paper

EMBOSSING FOLDER

Technological advances and a group of very creative people have made pressed embossing much easier. Using an embossing folder (a piece of molded plastic with a male and a female side) gives you a well-defined embossed image. As long as you have the machine, it's a fast way to emboss.

1 Emboss the 5½ x 8½-inch (14 x 21.6 cm) sheet of card stock by inserting it into the embossing folder and roll it through the die-cutting machine.

2 With a ruler and penknife on a cutting mat, crop the embossed card stock to 5 x 5 inches (12.5 x 12.5 cm). Create the frame by cutting a 1-inch (2.5 cm) margin.

3 Cut the printed message using the flourished cutting die. Place the die over the printed message and roll through the die-cutting machine.

4 Adhere the frame to the folded card with foam adhesive squares. Center the die cutout and secure by folding over the right and left edges and adhere to the back of the front panel with adhesive. Add the pearl embellishments to the center of this cutout.

Wax Paper Helps

Use a sheet of wax paper between the cutting die and card stock to help intricate patterns release from the die.

FAUX LETTER PRESS

Flat plastic (Mylar) stencils are easy to use especially when coloring with inks and paints. They have enough thickness (as thin as they are) to go through a die-cutting machine with subtle yet impressive results.

1

3

1

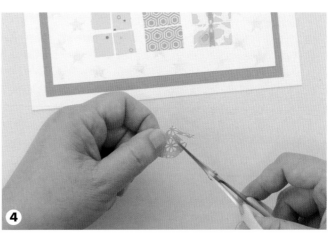

4

2

2

5

1 To slightly emboss the white card stock, layer the stencil over it and, using the correct recipe of shims, run it through the die-cutting machine.

2 Add color to the embossed image by masking the background with the stencil and applying color to the image with the ink pad.

3 To illustrate the gift packages, starting from the left image, cut four ½-inch (1.3 cm) squares of decorative masking tape and position in a square block. Next, cut three 1-inch (2.5 cm) horizontal strips of the second tape and stack on

top of each other, leaving a 1 mm gap. Finally, cut two 1-inch (2.5 cm) strips of the third tape and align vertically.

4 Create the bows by cutting a ¾-inch (2 cm) piece from contrasting colored tape and create a fringe by cutting 2 mm slices. Be sure not to cut through the entire piece.

5 Apply the bows to the tops of the packages.

6 Assemble the card by adhering to the pink card stock and adhere to the folded note card.

YOU WILL NEED

- 1 sheet aluminum foil, 6 x 7 inches (15.2 x 17.8 cm)
- double-sided tape
- 1 strip decorative paper, ½ x 5½ inches (1.3 x 14 cm)
- 1 sheet blue card stock, 5½ x 4¼ inches (14 x 10.8 cm)
- 1 folded note card, 5½ x 8½ inches (14 x 21.6 cm)
- adhesive
- 1 metal charm
- 1 stencil (Mylar) of fancy trellis
- die-cutting machine
- scissors

EMBOSSED KITCHEN SUPPLIES

Reduce, reuse, recycle—right? Embossed metals are extremely elegant, as shown in the metal repoussé card, but different metals may be a little too valuable for ordinary greeting cards.

Dig into the kitchen cabinet and with the help of a stencil (or embossing folder) and personal die-cutting machine, no one will suspect that sheet of aluminum foil or recycled soda can is not silver or pewter.

1 Layer the sheet of aluminum foil and the stencil into your die-cutting machine. Roll through the machine.

2 Carefully cut the foil to measure 5½ x 3¾ inches (14 x 9.5 cm). Apply double-sided tape to the foil.

3 Adhere the paper strip to the front of the foil layer with a thin strip of double-sided tape.

4 Adhere the foil to the blue card stock and finally onto the folded card. Glue on a metal charm to complete the card.

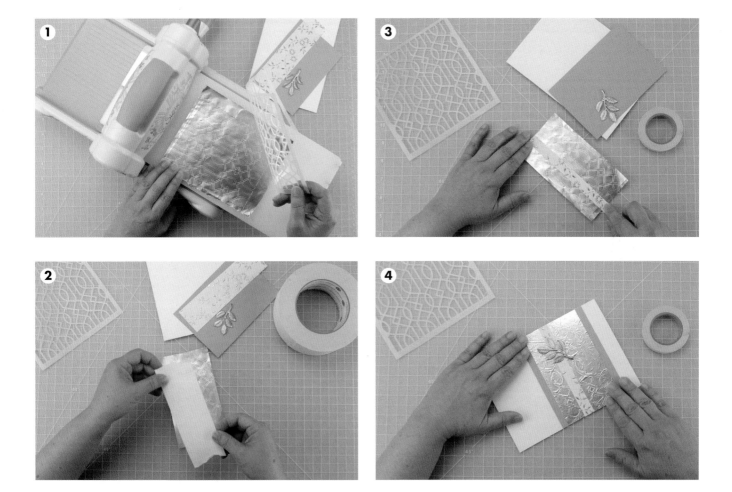

Aluminum Can Art

Grab that can before it goes into the recycle bin. Cut off the top and bottom and cut again lengthwise to square it up a bit. Roll it through a die-cutting machine and embossing folder and wow.

RUBBER STAMP EMBOSSING

This style of embossing is sometimes known as "poor man's engraving" or heat embossing. It is a process developed in the early 1900s that simulates engraved greeting cards. Instead of producing costly engraved plates, where paper is pressed and printed, creating a raised image, heat embossing is the process where a plastic powder is dusted over stamped wet ink and the excess is removed. Heat is applied and melts the powder, leaving a raised printed image.

YOU WILL NEED

- 1 red folded note card, 4 x 6 inches (10 x 15.2 cm)
- pigment or embossing ink
- metallic gold embossing powder
- 1 sheet red card stock, 4 x 6 inches (10 x 15.2 cm)
- mini double-sided adhesive foam squares
- rubber stamps of a long border and a bow
- heat tool
- scissors

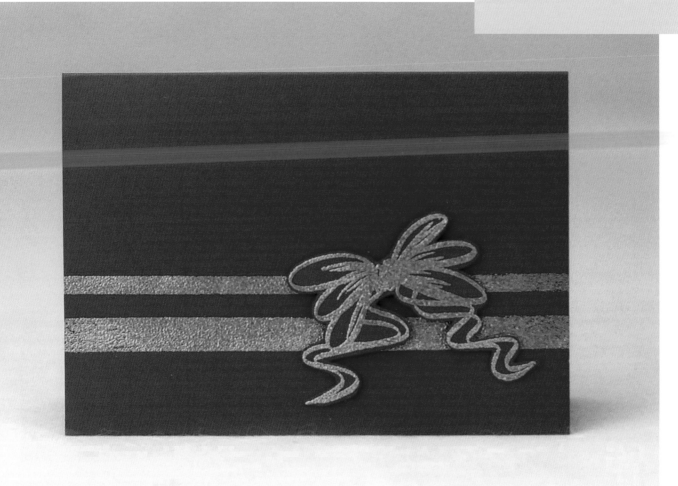

Inks and Powders

Embossing with rubber stamps is great if you have the right tools: dry powder, wet ink, and heat. It seems obvious, but embossing powders can absorb moisture and ink pads can dry up. Test different combinations because you cannot tell just by looking at the containers. If all else fails, make sure you are using pigment ink (which stays wet longer) or an ink recommended for embossing.

1 Stamp the bow onto the red card stock with pigment or embossing ink.

2 Dust the metallic gold embossing powder over the wet ink. Shake off the excess powder and return to the jar. Secure the lid.

3 Melt the powder with the heat tool.

4 Cut out the image and set aside.

5 Stamp and emboss the border image horizontally onto the folded note card.

6 Adhere the bow onto the embossed border image with mini double-sided adhesive foam squares.

Stamping Techniques

Making cards that are stamped is great because once you compose the card's layout, you can use these stamping techniques to duplicate your card as many times as you wish. However, keep in mind that it is perfectly wonderful to have a stamped card that is one of a kind.

SIMPLY STAMPING

There's an elegance to simplicity. It's just one image that creates the border.

YOU WILL NEED

- 1 sheet pink card stock, 3 ¾ x 3 inches (9.5 x 7.5 cm)

- plum ink pad

- self-adhesive pearl embellishments

- adhesive

- 1 sheet light plum card stock, 3 ¾ x 3 ½ inches (9.5 x 8.9 cm)

- 1 plum folded note card, 3 ¾ x 8 ⅝ inches (9.5 x 22 cm)

- rubber stamp of pinwheel

Inking ABCs

You only need ink (or paint) and a stamp to create an image or a design. For best results when using a rubber stamp, tap the stamp gently on the surface of the ink pad to ensure even ink coverage on the rubber. I like to look at the stamp to make sure there is enough ink on the rubber. Press the inked side gently but firmly onto a smooth piece of paper. Be sure to clean off the ink when changing colors, especially if switching from dark to light colors. Most inks can be cleaned with water; however, permanent inks (solvent based) need solvent cleaners. For best results, use ink cleaner to help remove all of the ink.

Applying Small Jewel Embellishments

Pick up small flat-backed rhinestones or pearls with a little beeswax on the end of a small bamboo skewer or a wax pencil.

1 With the pink card stock positioned horizontally on your work surface, stamp the pinwheel image in a horizontal line. It is okay if the images touch or overlap.

2 Adhere the pearl embellishments in the center of the images.

3 Adhere to the light plum card stock and then adhere to the folded notecard.

COLORFUL BACKGROUNDS

There are times when I need a decorative background paper for a project. Stamping your own paper ensures the colors will match. You can turn a white sheet of paper into a colorful explosion of fun.

YOU WILL NEED

- dye-based ink pads, pink, orange, and yellow
- 1 white folded note card, 5 x 7 inches (12.5 x 17.8 cm)
- 1 sheet white card stock, 4¼ x 5½ inches (10.8 x 14 cm)
- black solvent-based ink pad
- adhesive
- 1 sheet green card stock, 4 x 2¾ inches (10 x 7 cm)
- rubber stamps of a cherry blossom, cotton fluff, and bicycle
- rubber stamp cleaner
- paper trimmer
- markers, yellow, magenta, and orange

1. Rubber stamp the cherry blossom in pink ink onto the white note card. Stamp in a diamond pattern and off the edges of the card. Clean the ink off the stamp and change to orange color. Stamp more cherry blossoms.

2. Stamp the cotton fluff stamp in yellow ink, filling in the blank areas of the folded card. Set aside.

Stamping a Pattern

Stamp your image somewhere in the middle of the card and work in a "checkerboard pattern," making sure to stamp some of the images off the edges of the paper. You can add several images in the same design, but use different colors.

Stop the Bleeding

Stamping with permanent or solvent-based ink and coloring with water-based markers will not bleed. The opposite is true when using permanent ink markers. Use dye-based inks to stamp and permanent markers will not bleed the stamped image.

3. Stamp the bicycle onto the white card stock with the solvent-based ink. Crop with a ½-inch (1.3 cm) margin or to approximately 3½ x 2¼ inches (8.9 x 5.7 cm). Color little dots of yellow, orange, and magenta in the basket on the bicycle with markers.

4. Adhere to the green card stock and adhere to the colorfully stamped folded card.

YOU WILL NEED

- pigment or embossing ink

- 1 sheet decorative card stock, 4¼ x 5½ inches (10.8 x 14 cm)

- black embossing powder

- 1 scrap white card stock

- 1 strip white card stock, ¼ x 4¼ inches (6 mm x 10.8 cm)

- adhesive

- 1 white folded note card, 4¼ x 5½ inches (10.8 x 14 cm)

- rubber stamp of background image of flowers and butterflies

- heat tool

- rubber stamp of butterfly

- markers

- scissors

- penknife

- cutting mat

ONE STAMP BACKGROUND

Working backward can often lead to beautiful and interesting results. With this card, you'll create the background paper by stamping on top of a colorful paper.

1 Stamp the background image with pigment ink onto the decorative card stock.

2 Pour the black embossing powder on top of the wet ink and shake off the excess; return to the jar.

3 Use the heat tool to melt the powder.

4 Stamp the single butterfly onto the scrap card stock and color in with markers.

5 Cut out with scissors.

6 With a penknife and cutting mat, cut two ⅜-inch (1 cm) slices about ¼ inch (6 mm) apart on the butterfly

cutout. This will create the opening for the strip of card stock.

7 Thread the paper strip through the double slices to create a band with the butterfly working like a buckle.

8 Adhere to the stamped background and adhere to the folded card.

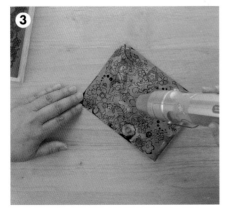

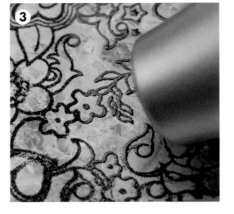

FINGERPRINT STAMPING

There's no better tool than the tips of your fingers. They are easy to clean, do not require a special purchase, and are easy to find. Use bright-colored inks and a pen for added detail to make many different cards.

YOU WILL NEED

- aqua ink pad
- 1 sheet white card stock, 8 x 5¼ inches (20 x 13.4 cm)
- 1 light blue folded note card, 4¼ x 5½ inches (10.8 x 14 cm)
- adhesive
- ruler
- fine-point pen
- bone folder

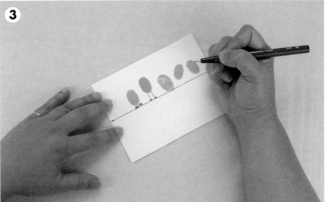

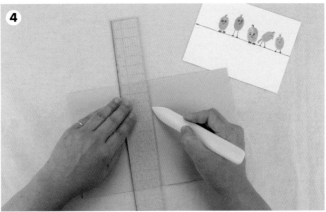

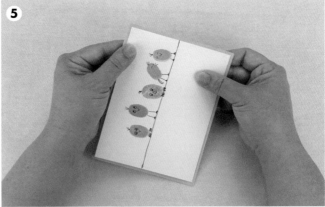

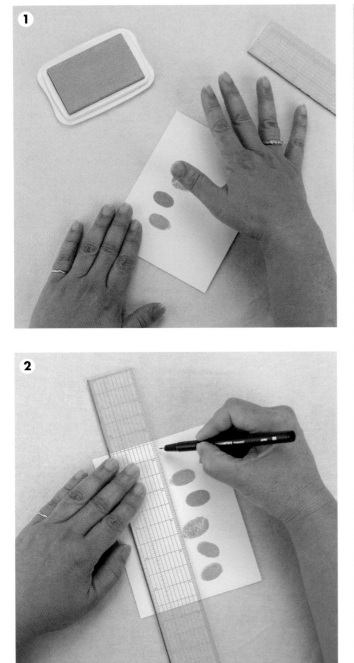

1 Ink your index finger with aqua-colored ink. Press your inked finger onto the white card stock approximately one-third from the top of the card. Repeat using your thumb to create a larger image.

2 Align a ruler near the bottoms of the fingerprints, and draw a line extending the length of the card.

3 Using the fine-point pen, draw eyes onto the fingerprints as well as legs and feet. Set aside.

4 Score the blue card stock in half to make a crisp folded card.

5 Adhere the fingerprint-bird layer to the folded card.

YOU WILL NEED

- 1 sheet white card stock, 4 x 4½ inches (10 x 11.5 cm)

- ink pads, pink, magenta, orange, and cyan blue

- 1 Inchie (thick and sturdy card stock), 1 x 1 inch (2.5 x 2.5 cm)

- double-sided foam squares

- bookmark tassel

- adhesive

- 1 white folded note card, 4 x 5 inches (10 x 12.5 cm)

- rubber stamps of mod mum and daisy

- permanent ink markers, black, cyan blue, and orange

TEENY WEENY INCHIE

These little 1-inch (2.5 cm) squares are made from high-end, thick card stock. It works perfectly with all media, creating little works of art that can be adhered to your cards. But more important than these little Inchies is how to stamp a large image onto this teeny weeny piece.

1. Stamp the mum image onto the white card stock in pink, magenta, orange, and cyan blue. Set aside.

2. Stamping the daisy onto the Inchie is tricky. This is because you cannot see where you are placing the stamp on this teeny piece. The way to stamp a large image onto a small piece of paper is to flip everything over. Turn the rubber stamp so the rubber is facing up. Using a black ink marker, color only the flower. You can ignore the stem.

3. Position the Inchie over the inked stamp and press the Inchie to the rubber. Carefully lift off the inked Inchie. This works because the Inchie is thick and will not deform when you press it to the stamp.

4. Color the flower petals with permanent ink markers.

5. Add a tassel. With the Inchie face down on your work surface, turn it a quarter turn. Apply two foam squares above and two foam squares below the center point, leaving an 1/8 inch (3 mm) gap. You've just created a channel for the cord of the tassel.

6. Lay the cord of the tassel between the foam squares with the fringe of the tassel hanging over the edge.

Shorten It Up

If the loop of the tassel is too long, tie a simple knot and extend it over the edge of the Inchie. It looks neater and adds a little interest.

7. Remove the backing from the foam tape and adhere the Inchie to the stamped card stock.

8. Adhere the card stock to the folded card.

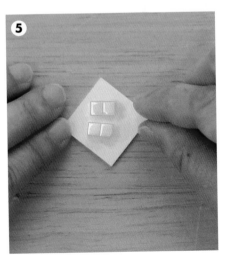

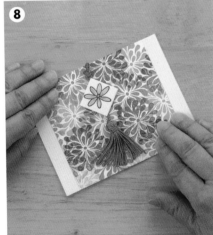

OUTLINE-STYLE STAMPS

Generally, an outline rubber stamp image looks best when stamped with black ink and colored in. There are so many options for adding the color—colored pencils, dye ink markers, permanent ink markers, watercolors, and chalks, to name a few. With whatever coloring tool you prefer, this style of cardmaking reminds me of the coloring books and crayons that were my favorite birthday or holiday gift.

1 Stamp lilies onto the white card stock with black dye-based ink.

2 Color with permanent ink markers. Start with light colors and blend in the darker colors.

3 Add highlights of white and gold to the lily petals.

4 Crop to ¼-inch (6 mm) margin, which is approximately 3¼ x 4¼ inches (8.3 x 10.8 cm). Adhere to the decorative card stock and adhere to the folded card.

Opposites Work

When using markers to color stamped images, there is chance of smearing the black ink. If you understand which inks work together, then the smearing will be minimal. When stamping with dye-based ink, use permanent (aka solvent- or alcohol-based) markers. The opposite is also true: If using permanent ink to stamp your design, use dye-based (water-based) inks and paints to color. Dry media (crayons, chalk, or colored pencils) are popular because any base ink will not smear. Yeah!

YOU WILL NEED

- 1 sheet white card stock, 4 x 5 inches (10 x 12.5 cm)
- 1 white folded note card, 5 x 7 inches (12.5 x 17.8 cm)
- 1 decorative tassel with 7-inch (14 cm) loop
- adhesive
- 1 sheet blue card stock, 4½ x 5½ inches (11.4 x 14 cm)
- rubber stamp of cherry blossom
- dye ink markers, magenta, plum, light blue, salvia blue, pale violet, and violet
- hole punch, 1/16 inch (1.5 mm)
- scissors

SOLID IMAGE RUBBER STAMPS WITH MARKERS

There are many ways to apply color to paper using a rubber stamp. Felt-tipped dye-based markers are versatile, are easy to use, and yield nice results.

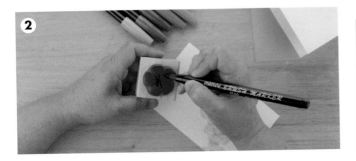

1 Color the rubber stamp with markers using two colors of ink. Starting with the light color first, complete coloring the image.

2 Add the darker color in the area you choose. For this image, the center of the flower should be darker. Stamp onto the white card stock.

3 You can get a second impression without inking your stamp, but the image will be faded. This looks great because it adds to the feeling of dimension, with the lighter image giving the appearance of being in the distance.

Which Colors to Add When

If using different colors of ink on one stamp image, it can be confusing which color to use first. Generally, it is best to start with the lighter color first and apply the darker color next. The tip of the marker will pick up a little of the previous ink, and the darker color mixed with a little of the lighter color is less noticeable.

4 To add the tassel around the fold of the card, start by punching two 1⁄16-inch (1.5 mm) holes 1 inch (2.5 cm) from the edge and along the center fold of the note card.

5 Cut from the edge to the punched hole.

6 Loop the tassel over one panel of the card and cinch it snug with the sliding braided ball.

7 Adhere the stamped card stock to the blue card stock and adhere to the folded card.

Painted

Applying color to paper always makes for a wonderful surprise. Add water to dry paint, then splatter. Drop or brush watercolor paint onto a piece of paper and you have the start of a greeting card.

SPOTS AND SPLATTER
Creating Spots

1 With an eyedropper, add 5 to 10 drops of water to water-color paint (for this project light colors look best) and mix carefully with a paintbrush. Fill the eyedropper with approximately 2 ml of paint.

2 Place 5 to 7 drops of paint onto the watercolor paper. Let air dry or use a hair dryer to speed drying. If using a hair dryer, hold at a distance so airflow is slower and does not spread the paint.

3 Repeat this step using different colors, letting each color dry before adding the next color.

Creating Splatter

1 Spread newspaper onto a work surface and wear an apron, if desired.

2 Load the paintbrush with watercolor paint (darker colors look best for this project).

3 Hold a chopstick or pencil (with your less dominate hand) over the painted paper. Tap the loaded paintbrush onto the chopstick and the paint will spatter.

4 Let the paint dry and crop to 4½ x 7¼ inches (11.4 x 18.1 cm). Adhere to the folded note card.

Direction of Splatter

You can direct the paint splatters by angling the paintbrush or chopstick over the watercolor paper. The size of the splatter can be controlled by the pressure or strength of tapping the paint-brush onto the chopstick.

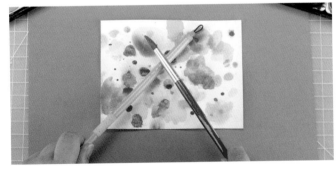

PAINTED STRIPES

YOU WILL NEED

- 1 sheet watercolor paper

- adhesive

- 1 sheet black card stock, 2¼ x 5 inches (5.7 x 12.5 cm)

- 1 folded note card, 3¾ x 8½ inches (9.5 x 21.6 cm)

- medium round bristle paintbrush (#5 up to #8)

- watercolors

- paper trimmer

1. With a paintbrush, apply paint in a horizontal strip approximately 1 inch (2.5 cm) deep across the watercolor paper.

2. Change the color of paint to the next shade and repeat this step down the length of the paper. Let dry.

3. Crop the paper to 2 x 4¾ inches (5 x 12.1 cm) and adhere to the black card stock, then adhere to the folded card.

How Much Water?

It is okay to use a generous amount of water. This allows pigments to puddle and later create darker and lighter shades when dry.

PAINTED STRIPES, WOOD GRAIN VARIATION

Create the appearance of wood grain by using shades of brown watercolors.

1 Load the brush with brown paint and dip into water to supersaturate the brush. Apply the paint horizontally across the watercolor paper. Allow the paint to puddle in areas as well as fade. These are created with too much water. Let dry.

2 Using a fine-point permanent marker or a sharp pencil tip, draw a line along the darkest part of the stripe. For best results, draw the line at the intersection of dark and light to separate the parts of the stripe.

3 Crop to 5¼ x 4 inches (13.3 x 10 cm), choosing the best areas of painted wood grain.

4 Adhere to the black folded card.

5 Use a corner rounder to round the corners of the black and cream-colored card stocks. Adhere the black rectangle to the cream-colored card stock and write "Thank You" with white marker.

6 Adhere to the folded card.

YOU WILL NEED

- 1 postcard-size sheet smooth watercolor paper
- adhesive
- 1 sheet black card stock, at least ½ inch (1.3 cm) larger than rubber stamp image
- 1 white folded note card, 5½ x 5½ inches (14 x 14 cm)
- rubber stamp of poppy in square outline
- black permanent ink stamp pad
- watercolors
- medium round bristle paintbrush (#5 up to #8)
- ruler
- penknife
- cutting mat

PAINTED STAMPED IMAGE

Creating a watercolor greeting is fast if you only have to color in an image that is already drawn for you. This is where rubber stamps work nicely. It is often difficult to print or transfer an illustration onto watercolor paper, but stamping the design is fast and easy.

1 Stamp the image with black permanent ink onto the water-color paper. Let dry.

2 Paint the image using lighter colors first and letting each color dry before applying the next color.

3 Crop the image with a ruler and penknife on a cutting mat, then adhere to the black card stock.

4 Adhere the layer to the folded note card.

No Measuring Frame

1 A quick way to cut a frame without measuring is to stamp the image onto the framing paper.

2 In this case, the paper is black, which is a little hard to see, but surprisingly you can.

3 Using the guidelines on the ruler, align along the edges of the paper and using the penknife, trim away.

LOOSELY COLORED STAMPED IMAGE

For variation, stamp an outline-style image and loosely color with watercolor paints.

YOU WILL NEED

- 1 sheet watercolor paper, 5 x 6 inches (12.5 x 15.2 cm)

- black pigment ink stamp pad

- clear embossing powder

- rubber stamp of Christmas ornament

- heat tool

- watercolors

- medium round bristle paintbrush (#5 up to #8)

- chopstick, pencil, or spare paintbrush

Speed It Up

You can use a hair dryer to speed drying, but diffuse air over wet watercolors, as direct air may make the paint run.

1 Stamp the image onto the watercolor paper with black pigment ink. Cover with clear embossing power. Shake off the excess and return to the bottle. Set with a heat tool.

2 Paint the background around the images starting with a light color. Load the paintbrush with water and a small amount of paint. This gives you the appearance of pastel or lighter colors. Let dry.

3 Start working on the focus images. For this style, it is okay to be a little sloppy, but not too much. Continue with the next color, again allowing the paint to dry.

4 Add some texture by splattering a darker color of paint by tapping the brush on a chopstick.

YOU WILL NEED

- 1 sheet watercolor paper, 4¼ x 5½ inches (10.8 x 14 cm)

- adhesive

- 1 sheet colored card stock, 5 x 5 inches (12.5 x 12.5 cm)

- 1 white folded note card, 5½ x 5½ inches (14 x 14 cm)

- pencil

- ruler

- fine-tip permanent pen

- watercolors

- medium round bristle paintbrush (#5 up to #8)

- penknife

- cutting mat

PAINTED SKETCHED DOODLES

Do you doodle? If yes, this card is easy. If not, read on. You will see how fun this is, and wait until you send this card. Everyone will be impressed.

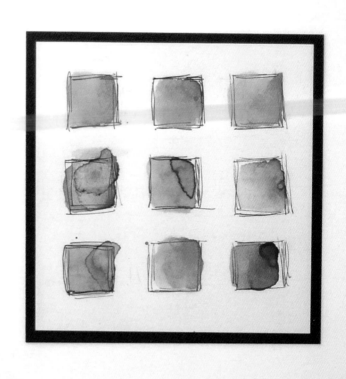

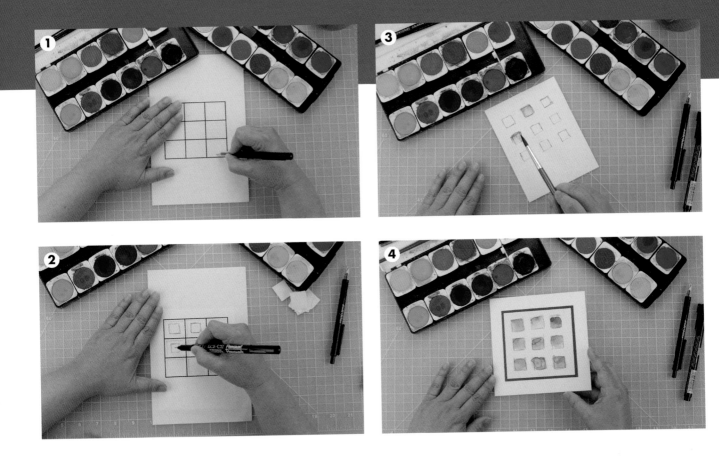

1. With a pencil and ruler, lightly draw a tic-tac-toe grid (nine equal squares) onto the watercolor paper, leaving a ½-inch (1.3 cm) margin.

2. Using the permanent pen, sketch one square in each tic-tac-toe square that is smaller than the grid guide. It is okay to draw the squares more than one time. This gives the doodle a sketched look.

3. Paint the square doodles using a variety of colors. For best results, choose three colors in one or two color families.

4. Crop the image with the penknife and ruler on a cutting mat or with a paper trimmer and adhere to the colored card stock. Crop the colored card stock so the image is framed with a ⅛-inch (3 mm) margin. Adhere the layer to the note card.

Painted Sketched Image, Variations

You don't have to stop with squares. Try other shapes like circles and hearts.

ABSOLUTELY RESISTING

Wax repels water. Enough said. Applying wax to the paper surface creates a barrier to watercolor paints. Pull out your crayons, scribble, and let the resisting begin.

YOU WILL NEED

- 1 sheet white card stock, 5 x 5 inches (12.5 x 12.5 cm)

- adhesive

- 1 sheet decorative card stock, 5 x 5 inches (12.5 x 12.5 cm)

- 1 folded note card, 5½ x 5½ inches (14 x 14 cm)

- 1 wax crayon

- watercolors (metallic)

- paintbrush

- paper trimmer

Variation

1 Spread about a pea-size amount of paste wax (micro glaze) onto the scrap paper. Spread evenly into a thin layer until the depth equals the card stock thickness.

2 "Ink" the stamp by tapping it into the wax. Stamp the image onto the white card stock.

3 Finish this card as in steps 2–4 at left.

1 Draw or scribble an image onto the white card stock with the crayon.

2 Paint darker colors of watercolor over the crayon image.

3 Use a variation of colors for interest. Let dry.

4 Crop away any rough edges and adhere to the decorative card stock and finally onto the folded card.

OPAQUE PAINT ON COLORED PAPER

When you apply opaque paint to dark-colored papers, the pigments from the paint stand out on the paper, while normal watercolors (which are translucent) seem to disappear on dark papers. With this style, you can paint onto dark paper and by diluting the paint, you will achieve a feeling of dimension.

YOU WILL NEED

- black pigment ink pad
- 1 navy blue folded note card, 5½ x 5½ inches (14 x 14 cm)
- rubber stamp of outline of cabin in the woods (home for the holidays)
- acrylic paints
- paintbrush
- black embossing powder
- heat tool

1 Stamp the image onto the navy note card with black pigment and emboss with black embossing powder.

2 Paint with slightly diluted white acrylic paint onto areas that you wish to appear toward the foreground, or closer to you. Dip your paintbrush in water and continue painting in other areas.

3 Paint additional colors to complete the card.

Make Humps

If the outline of the image is embossed, it creates a domed, or humped, line. This makes a slight barrier, which helps keep the different colors of ink from running into each other.

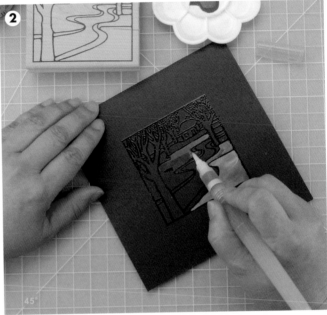

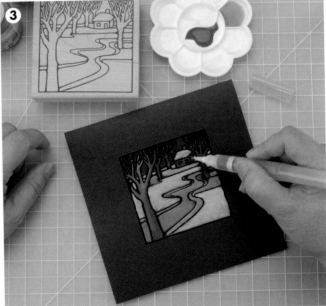

YOU WILL NEED

- 1 sheet white card stock, 5½ x 4¼ inches (14 x 10.8 cm)

- tissue paper in a variety of bright colors, yellow, light green, orange, violet, pink, light blue

- adhesive

- 1 rickrack-shaped band, 5½ inches (14 cm)

- 1 white folded note card, 5½ x 4¼ inches (14 x 10.8 cm)

- plastic tray

- paper towels

- paper trimmer

- spritzer bottle with water

- iron (optional)

- hair dryer (optional)

PAINTING WITH TISSUE PAPER

There are so many ways to add color to paper. I think this style of application was a happy accident.

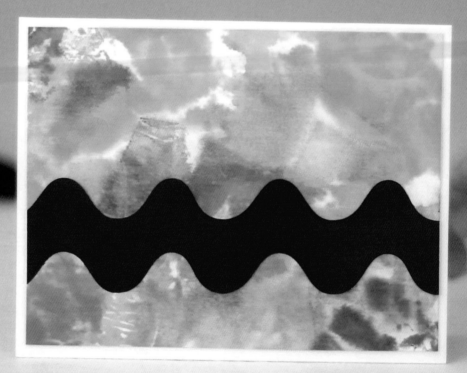

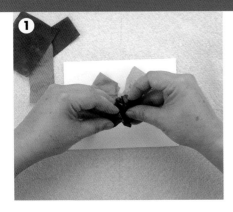

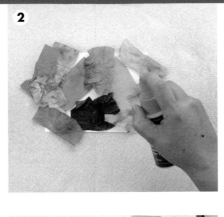

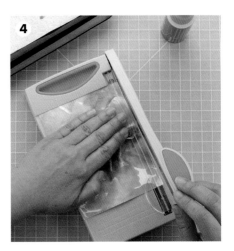

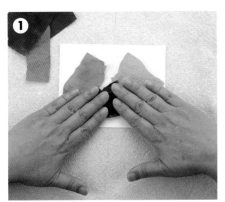

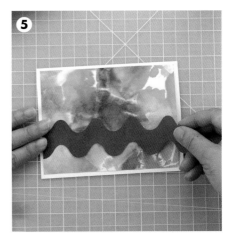

1 Cover the plastic tray with paper towels. Lay the sheet of card stock on top. Cut each sheet of tissue paper into smaller pieces. Crumple the tissue paper and scatter onto the card stock. Spread out, if you wish.

2 Spritz water over the tissue paper and saturate. If needed, press the paper down so all the wet surfaces touch the card stock. Let sit for several minutes. The longer you leave the wet tissues on the paper, the deeper the color transfer.

3 Remove the wet tissue paper. Let the card stock dry. Because the card stock will be saturated with water, it will curl as it dries. To flatten, iron the card stock between a couple of clean paper towels. Set the iron on medium heat. There will be a slight curl, but adhering it to the folded card will flatten it.

4 Trim the edges of the with a paper trimmer.

5 Adhere the rickrack band to the card stock and adhere to the folded card.

Efficient Cutting

Fold the tissue paper in half, then in half again, and continue until the sheet is approximately 5 x 7 inches (12.5 x 17.8 cm). Slide into your paper trimmer and cut off the folded edges and cut everything in half. You will have 32 or 64 pieces, depending on how small you make them.

Speedy Drying

For those of you who are impatient, you can speed the drying time with a hair dryer.

Suppliers

PRODUCT	SOURCE(S)	WEBSITE(S)
Adhesive, Diamond Glaze	JudiKins Inc.	www.judikins.com
Adhesive, Glue Square	ASI Kool Tak	http://asikooltak.com
Adhesive, glue stick	Elmer's	http://elmers.com
Adhesive, hot glue	AdTech	www.adhesivetech.com
Adhesive, metal	Beacon Adhesives	www.beaconadhesives.com
Adhesive, Mod Podge	Plaid Inc.	www.plaidonline.com
Adhesive, Perfect Paper	US Art Quest	http://artpapersonline.com
Bone Folder	JudiKins Inc.	www.judikins.com
Color wheel	ColorWheel Inc.	(Various sites)
Cutting dies	Sizzix, Spellbinder	www.sizzix.com, www.spellbinderspaperarts.com
Cutting mat	Marvy Uchida	www.uchida.com
Die cutting machine	Sizzix, Spellbinder	www.sizzix.com, www.spellbinderspaperarts.com
Embellishments, buttons	Blumenthal Lansing	www.buttonlovers.com
Embellishments, copper metal sheet	MercArt	www.mercartusa.com
Embellishments, Inchie	Inchie Arts, JudiKins Inc.	www.inchiearts.com, www.judikins.com
Embellishments, jewelry findings	Nunn Designs	http://nunndesign.com
Embellishments, mica tiles	US Art Quest	http://artpapersonline.com
Embellishments, paper cords	JudiKins Inc., Hanko	www.judikins.com, http://hankodesigns.com
Embellishments, paper flowers	US Art Quest	http://artpapersonline.com
Embellishments, rhinestones	Buckle Boutique	http://thebuckleboutique.com
Embellishments, tassels	JudiKins Inc.	www.judikins.com
Embellishments, washi tape	Bella Carta	http://bellacartaatartnsoul.blogspot.com
Embossing, folders	Sizzix	http://www.sizzix.com
Embossing, heat tool	Marvy Uchida	www.uchida.com
Embossing, powder	JudiKins Inc.	www.judikins.com
Glass beads	JudiKins Inc.	www.judikins.com
Ink pads	Clearsnap Inc., Tsukineko, Marvy Uchida	www.clearsnap.com, http://www.tsukineko.co.jp/english, www.uchida.com
Knife 11	Excel, Westcott	http://shop.excelblades.com, www.westcottbrand.com
Knife, pen	JudiKins Inc.	www.judikins.com
Paint brushes	Yasutomo	www.yasutomo.com

PRODUCT	SOURCE(S)	WEBSITE(S)
Paints, acrylic	Heindesign, Deco Arts	http://www.heindesign.de, http://decoart.com
Paints, mica watercolor palettes	US Art Quest, Yasutomo	http://artpapersonline.com, www.yasutomo.com
Paints, watercolor	Pelikan	www.pelikan.com
Paper, cardstock	JudiKins Inc.	www.judikins.com
Paper, handmade	US ArtQuest	http://artpapersonline.com
Paper, marbled	Skycraft Designs	www.skycraft.com
Paper, origami	Yasutomo, Aitoh	www.yasutomo.com, www.aitoh.com
Paper, printed	Paper Garden	www.papergardenboutique.com
Paper, rotary trimmer	Marvy Uchida	www.uchida.com
Paper, trimmer guillotine	Tonic Studios	https://tonic-gold.co.uk
Paper, vellum	Some Assembly Required	www.some-assembly-required.com
Paper, washi	Hanko, The Japanese Paper Place, Aiotoh, Moriki Paper	http://hankodesigns.com, www.japanesepaperplace.com, www.aitoh.com, http://morikipaper.com
Paper, wood veneer	Arc Crafts	www.arccrafts.com
Pencil, rhinestone picker	ASI Kool Tak	www.asikooltak.com
Pencils, colored	Lyra	http://pencils.com
Pens, fine-line	Sakura, Yasutomo	http://sakuraofamerica.com, www.yasutomo.com
Pens, markers	Marvy Uchida	www.uchida.com
Punches	Marvy Uchida, McGill, Yasutomo	www.uchida.com, www.mcgillinc.com/shop/pc/home.asp, www.yasutomo.com
Rubber stamps	JudiKins Inc., Heindesign	www.judikins.com, http://heindesign.de
Ruler, clear	JudiKins Inc.	www.judikins.com
Scissors, 6-inch (15.2 cm)	Westcott	www.westcottbrand.com
Scissors, detail	JudiKins Inc.	www.judikins.com
Scoring board	Crafter's Companion, Scor-It	http://crafterscompanion.com
Stencils	Kite Stencils	http://kitestencil.com
Tape, double-sided	ASI Kool Tak	http://asikooltak.com
Tape, mosaic	JudiKins Inc.	www.judikins.com
Tool, Pergamano	Some Assembly Required	www.some-assembly-required.com
Tool, quilling	Quilled Creations	http://quilledcreations.com
Window plastic	JudiKins Inc.	www.judikins.com

Glossary

COLLAGE: A work of art created by gluing various pieces together on a single backing.

COMPLEMENTARY COLORS: These colors are opposite on the color wheel and create dramatic and eye-popping visuals.

COMPOSITION: Organization and arrangement of various elements to create a whole product.

CONTRASTING COLORS: Also known as complementary colors, these are colors opposite, or far apart, on the color wheel.

CROPPING: To cut off the edges of a photograph or piece of paper.

EPHEMERA: Items intended to be used for a short period of time, like tickets, postcards, and newspaper clippings.

FOREGROUND: The part of the image closest to the observer.

GRAIN: Fibers aligned in a certain direction to create a piece of paper.

INCHIE: A 1 x 1-inch (2.5x2.5 cm) piece of paper.

LANDSCAPE (ALIGNMENT OF PAPER): Horizontal, an image wider than it is tall.

MIZUHIKI: Decorative paper cords that are traditionally Japanese and made with washi paper, which is dyed for color and stiffened with starch.

MONOCHROMATIC: Containing one color or a variety of shades of one color.

PORTRAIT (ALIGNMENT OF PAPER): Vertical, an image taller than it is wide.

RULE OF THIRDS: The concept of imagining a tic-tac-toe board over the image, and then placing the focus of the card along the lines or intersections of the lines.

SQUARING UP: Taking an asymmetrical piece of paper and cutting all four sides to create a clean square.

TWINCHIE: A 2 x 2-inch (5 x 5 cm) piece of paper.

Iris Folding Pattern

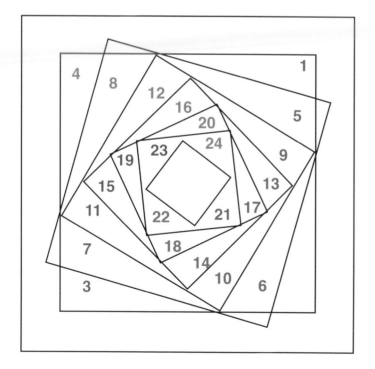

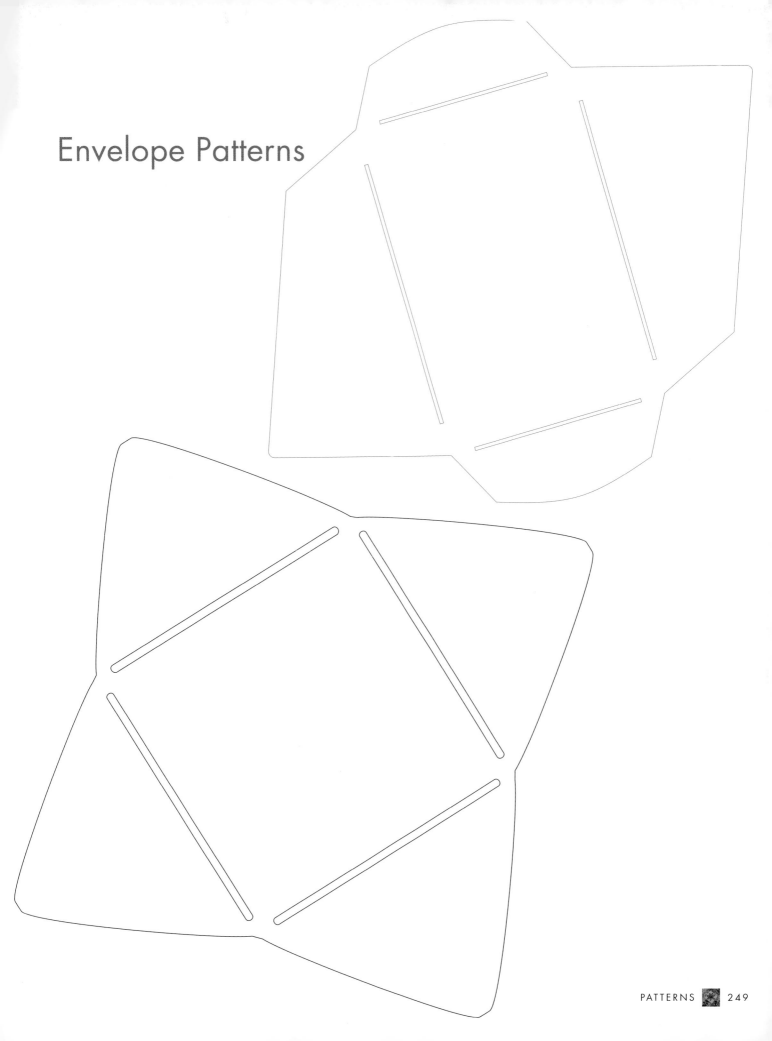

Envelope Patterns

Yin Yang Heart Pattern

About the Author

Judi Watanabe's love for card making started as soon as she was tall enough to reach the mailbox. Learning to carve erasers led to her next passion, rubber stamping. Together with her husband, Rob, she grew JudiKins Rubber Stamps from a small business in their garage in 1989 to one of the most innovative craft product manufacturers in the industry today. Judi now travels the world teaching and demonstrating rubber stamping techniques with projects that strive to reflect her philosophy of "simple elegance."

Acknowledgments

The creation of this book could not have been possible without the wonderful circle of family, and friends who fill my "creative bank". Rob, Mom, Dad, Liz, Joyce, Cherryl, Sharon, Kat, MaryJo, Sarah, Ana, Wolfgang, Peggy, Jacqueline, Dee and Cdub have all played an important part in its creation. They have, advised, consulted and corrected, but mostly they just gave me that encouraging nudge when I needed it.

A super special thanks to the Creative Publishing international team for being so patient and supportive. And to everyone at JudiKins, thanks for keeping the rubber stamps flowing while I made lots of cards.

Index

Quarto is the authority on a wide range of topics.

Quarto educates, entertains and enriches the lives of our readers—enthusiasts and lovers of hands-on living.

www.QuartoKnows.com

Also Available from Quarto Publishing Group USA

Cards That Wow with Sizzix

ISBN: 978-1-58923-884-8

Make It a Party with Sizzix

ISBN: 978-1-58923-933-3

Origami Boxes Super Paper Pack

ISBN: 978-1-58923-899-2

The Complete Photo Guide to Paper Crafts

ISBN: 978-1-58923-468-0

Playing with Paper

ISBN: 978-1-58923-814-0

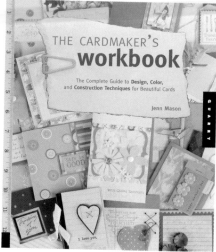

The Cardmaker's Workbook

ISBN: 978-1-58923-415-9